TORONTO

The Way We Were

TORONTO

The Way We Were

Mike Filey

DUNDURN PRESS
Toronto

Editor: Michael Carroll
Copy-editor: Allison Hirst
Design and page layout: Kim Monteforte, WeMakeBooks.ca
Printer: Friesens

Library and Archives Canada Cataloguing in Publication

Filey, Mike, 1941–

Toronto : the way we were / by Mike Filey.

ISBN 978-1-55002-842-3

1. Toronto (Ont.)—History. I. Title.

FC3097.4.F548 2008   971.3'541   C2008-904410-X

1   2   3   4   5   12   11   10   09   08

Care has been taken to trace the ownership of copyright material used in this book. The author and the publisher welcome any information enabling them to rectify any references or credits in subsequent editions.

J. Kirk Howard, President

Printed and bound in Canada.

www.dundurn.com

Dundurn Press
3 Church Street, Suite 500
Toronto, Ontario, Canada
M5E 1M2

Gazelle Book Services Limited
White Cross Mills
High Town, Lancaster, England
LA1 4XS

Dundurn Press
2250 Military Road
Tonawanda, NY
U.S.A. 14150

Canada Council
for the Arts

Conseil des Arts
du Canada

Canadä

ONTARIO ARTS COUNCIL
CONSEIL DES ARTS DE L'ONTARIO

We acknowledge the support of **The Canada Council for the Arts** and the **Ontario Arts Council** for our publishing program. We also acknowledge the financial support of the **Government of Canada** through the **Book Publishing Industry Development Program** and **The Association for the Export of Canadian Books**, and the **Government of Ontario** through the **Ontario Book Publishers Tax Credit** program, and the **Ontario Media Development Corporation**.

This collection of stories is dedicated to
Toronto's own Marilyn Bell Di Lascio and
to the memory of her late husband, Joe.

Contents

Foreword by the Honourable David C. Onley, Lieutenant Governor
    of Ontario   13

Foreword by David Crombie: Walking Toronto's Waterfront   17

Acknowledgements   21

Introduction   23

1 **TORONTO'S PASSING SCENE   27**

   Birth of a City   28

   Many Happy Returns   29

   Our Mother of Invention   32

   The CNE That Was ...   34

   Postcard Perfect   35

   Torn from the Headlines   36

   Water Tanks ... for the Memories   38

   On the Beat Since 1834   40

   Grab Your Easter Bonnet   42

   Celebrations in History   44

   History of Improvement   46

   The Bells, the Bells   48

   Ring in the New Year   49

   Calling 1947!   50

   Mayor Foster's Care   52

The Toronto Girl "Tobogganing"

2 TORONTO'S WAR YEARS 55

Days of Defeat   56

Path to a Great Tribute   57

In Praise of Our Heroes   59

It's Over, Over There   61

An Anniversary of Note   63

3 TORONTO PLEASURE PALACES 65

Kicking Up Our Heels   66

The Palais Royale Reborn   67

Casino Royale   69

Coulda Danced All Night   71

The Play's the Thing   73

On the Sunnyside   74

The Gardens   76

More Power For Ontario

Hydro's Richard L. Hearn Generating Station goes into operation at Toronto

4 TORONTO AT WORK 79

A Hit, One Tire at a Time   80

Banking on Canada   82

Driving Ambition   83

Not at Your Service   85

Public Power   87

Snapshot of the Past   89

Luxury Up on High   91

Gas Pains   93

5 TORONTO AND DISASTER 97

Our City in Ruins   98

Rare Photos of the Great Toronto Fire   99

Toronto's Worst Disaster   101

Up in Smoke   103

Watery Grave   105

Swept Away   106

6 TORONTO LANDMARKS 109

Toronto's Tower of Power   110

Pray in Beauty   111

Postal Past   113

Prime Real Estate   114

Save the Roundhouse   116

The Flatiron Building   118

T.O. Streets Full of Art   120

A House Like No Other   122

A Pleasant Walk in the Past   124

And the Winner Was ...   125

Battle for Sunnybrook   127

Child Full of Grace   129

Defending Fort York   130

Doing Time in T.O.   131

Fanciful Flights   133

Mi Casa Loma   134

Milestones in Medicine   137

7 TORONTO THEN AND NOW 139

On the Banks of the Don   140

Capsule Moment   141

On the Wharf   142

City at the Crossroads   144

Pride of Ownership   146

Facelift for Toronto's Central Piazza   148

Historic Home on the Move   149

Once Around the Park   151

Streetcars on Track   153

8 TORONTO ON THE MOVE 157

Across the Bay   158

A Real-life Ferry Tale   160

Prowling the Waters   162

Flights of Fancy   163

Airport Was Slow to Fly   165

All Aboard the TTC   166

A Desire for Streetcars   169

Ball-oil or Ball-iol?   171

Happy Anniversary   172

Tunnel Vision   173

Bridges to the Past   175

9 TORONTO AT PLAY 177

Ex Marks the Spot 178

The Agony of Defeat 179

The Hockey Leafs Are Born 180

Streetcar to Swim Classes 182

10 TORONTO STREETSCAPES 185

Locked on the Grid 186

Aching with Memories 187

From Foe to Street Sign 189

Our Streets Are Paved in History 190

Streets Paved the Way 192

Stroll the Avenue 194

The Road to Riches 196

Top Drawer Streets 198

11 TORONTO NEIGHBOURHOODS 201

A Neighbourhood Tale 202

It's Déjà Vu for St. Clair 203

Yonge at Heart 205

Viaduct: A Mammoth Project 206

Toronto's Other Main Street 208

12 TORONTO WATERFRONT 211

On the Waterfront   212

Old Harbour Revisited   213

Island Fantasy   214

Across the Water and into the Air   215

Island Flights Take Off   217

Toronto Bay's Slow Roller   219

13 TORONTO FAMOUS AND CELEBRATED 221

And the Bands Played On   222

Oscar's First Toronto Show   223

That Miller Sound   225

Edward and the Ex   226

Marilyn Buoyed Our Hearts   228

Statue Honours Mary Pickford   230

Toronto Timeline   233

Image Captions for Part Titles   241

Foreword

by the Honourable David C. Onley, O.Ont., Lieutenant Governor of Ontario

Mike Filey is easily Toronto's best-known popular historian. Beginning with his first "The Way We Were" column in the *Toronto Sun* more than 35 years ago, Mike has shared his passion for this city with almost two generations of readers. For many of us, what we actually *know* about Toronto's past has been through Mike's articles and books. In fact, if you've lived in Toronto for a good part of your life, his stories invariably trigger personal memories or stories told to us by parents and grandparents. This newest volume of his work is no exception.

I suspect this is a fundamental part of Mike's appeal to us all. He is our city's storyteller, the uncle who has all those fascinating tidbits about our collective past. This is all the more important, since knowing where we've come from is crucial to understanding why we are where we are now and where we might be going tomorrow. Toronto, indeed, has changed greatly from the sleepy "Toronto the Good" of the 1950s to today's dynamic, multicultural centre of commerce and communications.

I remember those quieter times after our family moved to Toronto in 1957 when I was only seven years old. My mother and father loaded us into their 1956 Mercury Monarch station wagon and left my hometown of Midland just as the new school year was starting. They made the move so Dad could pursue his new position as deputy solicitor for the Township of Scarborough in the fledgling municipal experiment called Metropolitan Toronto, and so I could get the best treatment possible after contracting polio a few years earlier.

Along with my younger brother and sister, we arrived in West Hill near the Scarborough/Pickering border, thrilled to be living in our new home and excited to be near our beloved grandparents. Mostly, though, I knew I was leaving a small town and was going to be living in a big place, the city "with all the lights."

To me that's what Toronto was all about—a shimmering skyline of lights in the night. When we visited Toronto, as we often did before we moved there, my parents would leave Midland after work on Fridays, put us in the back of the station wagon, and take Highway 400 south to Toronto. Invariably, we would fall asleep along the way, but just north of the city, our folks would always wake us up when we got to that point where Toronto's skyline beckoned. Today, when I'm on Highway 400 at night heading back into the city, that illuminated outline of Toronto still triggers childhood travel memories—but, oh, how that skyline has changed!

For one thing, there was no CN Tower, known today around the world as Toronto's signature piece of architecture. There was no First Canadian Place, no TD Canada Trust Tower, no Royal Bank Plaza—none of the skyscrapers that give the skyline its unique look. Instead, the tallest building of the day, and for a time the tallest in the British Empire, was the Royal York Hotel, all 28 floors of it!

The sporting venues have changed, too. Maple Leaf Stadium at the foot of Bathurst Street was the home of the International League team that preceded the Blue Jays as Toronto's professional baseball team. It vanished long ago to be superseded by the retractable-roofed Rogers Centre. Exhibition Stadium, once the home of the Toronto Argonauts and the Blue Jays, featured a covered north grandstand and doubled as the city's largest outdoor all-purpose facility for the annual Canadian National Exhibition. Acts as diverse as Bob Hope, the Three Stooges, and Victor Borge performed there, but my favourite as a kid was the crash 'em, bash 'em stock car Hell Drivers. We knew as kids that *hell* was a bad word, and that they crashed cars, so it had to be a great show.

The hockey team I quickly lived for, of course, was the Maple Leafs, and their home rink, as Foster Hewitt would remind us every Saturday night, was Maple Leaf Gardens. Getting to a game was a rare treat, but in a time when television was black and white, seeing the teams' uniforms in full colour left an indelible memory.

Growing up in a small town, I wasn't used to modern highways. But to get to and from the CNE or Maple Leaf Gardens, my dad always sought out the two newest routes—the Don Valley Parkway and the Gardiner Expressway. The latter is now a topic of political debate, but in its day the Gardiner's unique lighting system seemed futuristic. The expressway's lights were built right into its safety railings, giving you the feeling of shooting through a space-age tunnel, especially if you were going up the Lake Shore Boulevard entrance ramp westbound from Leslie Street.

The DVP seemed equally futuristic as it wove through the Don Valley, its banked curves and ramps promising a quick-and-easy way in and out of the city. As a young auto enthusiast, I felt as if my dad were driving us in a racing car.

Now, of course, the parkway is dubbed the Don Valley Parking Lot, notions of speed long ago abandoned to practical utility. The Gardiner's futuristic lights have since been replaced by conventional light standards, and the Lake Shore entrance ramp near Leslie has given way to artistic concrete bridge supports, reminding us where the ramp was and what the Gardiner's future may be.

The Argos and the Blue Jays have decamped to Rogers Centre. Where Exhibition Stadium once stood is now the site of the crisp, clean BMO Field, home of the Toronto FC soccer team. Maple Leaf Gardens remains shuttered, its future uncertain, while the Leafs pursue that elusive next Stanley Cup from the still-beautiful Air Canada Centre.

Yet the city thrives, old places give way to modernity. Traditions such as the CNE, the Argos, and the Leafs remain, but in new buildings with new memories.

Through Mike Filey's latest work, *Toronto: The Way We Were*, the past is recalled though stories and pictures. We smile, we learn, we remember. Enjoy the memories. And sometime soon, check out Toronto's skyline. It continues to shimmer at night.

Foreword: Walking Toronto's Waterfront

by David Crombie

When Mike Filey asked me to make a contribution to *Toronto: The Way We Were*, I was in the process of planning a historical walking tour for the first annual Great Waterfront Trail Adventure. Organized by the Waterfront Regeneration Trust and part of Trails Open Ontario, this was a cyclists' celebration of Ontario's lakefront from Niagara to the Quebec border. Covering 414 miles and passing through 41 communities within eight days, it would be an ambitious and rewarding experience for over 150 riders. As for me, I've always been a walker, and as much as I can marvel at the many ways in which the Toronto portion of the trail can be enjoyed, it is by walking it that I most appreciate the city and its waterfront heritage.

Our walk begins at the nationally designated heritage site of Fort York because, after all, urban Toronto started out as a garrison town in 1793. In the shadow of a buried but hardly forgotten waterway, Garrison Creek, this outdoor museum continues to educate, inform, and make relevant for generations of Torontonians and visitors alike the city's early military beginnings and the significant role played by the fort in the War of 1812. When an important anniversary of that war is commemorated in 2012, Fort York will be at the centre of celebrations. As timeless as the appeal of interpreters in period costume and the explosive sound of the cannon are, it is the vibrancy of the site as it is used today that is remarkable. The museum's administrators, in a testament to their innovation, seem determined to sweep aside any hint of dust. Through dynamic programming and participation and partnership in activities such as the Great Waterfront Trail Adventure, which saw the Common littered with tents for over-nighting cyclists, they ensure that new narratives are acquired and our history continues to live and breathe.

Stopping at Bathurst Quay allows us to reflect on some of the signature developments of the 1970s and 1980s. Then Eb Zeidler brought new life to the waterfront, designing the "total environment" of a 90-acre park and playground. Ontario Place would complement the grounds of the Canadian National Exhibition, or "The Ex," as it is fondly known locally, enjoyed by residents since the first permanent fair was held there in 1879 under the auspices of the Toronto Industrial Exhibition. Farther east, visionaries created the Crown corporation of Harbourfront, a year-round centre for contemporary culture with imaginative programming spanning the realms of education, recreation, and the arts. Cutting-edge and ultra-modern at one time, these sites have now become part of our established lakefront.

Tellingly enough, it is by harkening farther back into the harbour's history that the landscape is once again being renewed and transformed. The iconic concrete silos of Canada Malting, which have stood here since 1928, are now framed by a limestone wall and the poignant stone sculptures of *The Arrival* of Ireland Park. Opened just last year, this beautiful yet moving spot honours the many Irish who came to Toronto in the 1840s after fleeing their native country's devastating famine. The silos themselves will play a significant role as keepers of the Toronto story, since that setting has been selected for a new city museum to be completed within the next decade.

Although the Bathurst Quay neighbourhood will no doubt take off with the addition of this development, we would do well to remember that this has been a point of "takeoff" for Torontonians in several senses for many generations. Between the mid-1920s and 1960s, well before the arrival of Rogers Centre, residents seeking to watch a baseball game on their day off would gather here at Maple Leaf Stadium. Long balls hit out of the park might even have landed in Norway—Little Norway, that is. A park with the same name now memorializes the wartime training camp of the Royal Norwegian Air Force. Indeed, though the number and size of aircraft at Toronto's City Centre Airport continue to provide the substance for heated debate, planes have been taking off from the waterfront almost since the dawn of modern flight and more formally when the island airfield was built in 1939 and named after King George VI.

The route to Spadina Quay is full of more recent efforts to link points of interest along the trail, while also enhancing opportunities for recreation and reflection at the water's edge. The Toronto Music Garden, an open-air venue within a natural landscape inspired by the music of Johann Sebastian Bach as interpreted by cellist Yo-Yo Ma, offers tours and concerts. HtO, an award-winning urban park, provides an easy yet dynamic meeting place. At the same time Waterfront Toronto continues to integrate heritage and contemporary use with its work at the Spadina slip head, where it is designing and building a series of connecting bridges compatible with the nautical history of the area.

York Quay is the site of what remains one of the city's most imaginative and beautiful undertakings when it comes to the adaptive re-use of derelict industrial space. Originally built in 1926, the Terminal Warehouse at one time provided a good 50 percent of the city's demand for storage space before it suffered the challenges of competition with other, newer warehouses, changed hands, and fell into disrepair prior to its purchase by the federal government. In 1983 the building was renovated and reincarnated as a retail and commercial concourse. Bathed in light and with a stunning view, it is a compelling and frequent waterfront destination for both tourists and city residents. Only a stone's throw away stands the 1907 Toronto Ferry Company Building, which has now found new purpose as an information kiosk for visitors. Due south, across the water and but a short trip from the ferry terminal at the bottom of Yonge Street, are the Toronto Islands. Six hundred acres of beauty, a natural playground, and a fantastic resource all too often taken for granted, the islands were cut loose from the mainland courtesy of a terrific storm in 1858. Sacred to aboriginal peoples for centuries, the islands remind us of a rich, yet still largely untold, history.

It is at the foot of Jarvis Street that one can see the last vestiges of Toronto the working port, including the Redpath Sugar Refinery, which still processes sugar from the Caribbean as it has since the 1950s. This frail and orphaned section of the waterfront cries out for attention and is scheduled to undergo transformative revitalization in the coming years. The Toronto waterfront's liberation from the Gardiner Expressway will begin here. That, together with the establishment of George Brown College's new campus for health sciences and a second urban park, Sugar Beach, which will comprise an urban beach, water's edge promenade, and granite-paved multi-functional event plaza, will serve to invigorate and animate the area once more.

Prior to the landfills that began in 1890, the city ended at Front Street. A surprising number of the structures and a strong sense of the streetscape of the Old Town, roughly from Yonge Street to River Street and extending from Queen Street down, remain. For almost two centuries the St. Lawrence Market has provided a meeting place for buyers and sellers. Nearby, and for nearly as long, St. James' Cathedral has beckoned Torontonians to worship, and one of Toronto's jewels of built heritage, the St. Lawrence Hall, has hosted concerts and lectures on issues of importance to each generation. Plans for a more comprehensive approach to restoration and regeneration of this historical precinct, arguably the most significant in the city, are underway, with a special interest in linking it to Union Station in the west and the Distillery District in the east in an easily accessible heritage trail. As we better understand the importance of our collective past and its role in our civic identity, the responsibilities imposed, and the opportunities offered through appropriate stewardship and creative and caring development, it becomes clear that this can only be achieved when public and private interests work together.

Farther east, at the bottom of another buried but much fabled watercourse called Taddle Creek, is the site of Toronto's first Parliament, a balancing companion piece to the better known Fort York in the west. Where the fort reminds us of a war won, a plaque commemorating an absent building demonstrates what can also be lost. A determined and loyal group of city archaeologists, local history buffs, and residents continues with its hopes and plans to establish a more visible and compelling means by which to celebrate this important aspect of the city's history.

We finish our walk at the Distillery District, another national historic site featuring North America's best and largest collection of industrial architecture of the Victorian era. Founded in the 1830s and at one time a major player in the nation's economic life, the Gooderham and Worts Distillery closed in 1990 due to a reduction in operations and the de-industrialization of the surrounding area. Fortunately, sensitive and imaginative redevelopment and restoration of the compound led to the opening, in 2003, of a pedestrian village full of restaurants, artists' studios and galleries, shops, and events programming. Now, far from derelict, the Distillery District is a vibrant terminus booming with activity.

Walking the waterfront where Toronto was born is a unique exercise in time travel. Its essential magic is the easy fluidity with which it connects past, present, and future—ever-changing yet ever-constant. This remarkable landscape that is a gift to our collective memory is at the same time sculpted and changed by our own profoundly personal experiences. It's a place where nature meets culture and where the imaginative shapes the physical as Toronto pursues its age-old hopes and dreams in a new century. Ours is an extraordinary legacy and a powerful opportunity. See you there ...

Acknowledgements

For more than 35 years my column "The Way We Were" has been a popular feature in the *Toronto Sun*. Here are a few of the people who, over those three-plus decades, have made that possible: Julie Kirsh, Kathy Webb-Nelson, Glenn Tapscott, Jillian Goddard, and Joyce Wagler in the *Toronto Sun* News Research Centre; Jim Thomson, Al Parker, Mike Burke-Gaffney, Ken Winlaw, and Bill Murray, who continue to make my columns read well and look nice; and Marilyn Figueroa, who ensures my remuneration is looked after.

I extend my thanks also to the two Davids—our lieutenant governor (and long-time friend), David Onley, and former Toronto mayor David Crombie, for their kind words. Thanks, as well, to Kirk Howard, Michael Carroll, Allison Hirst, and Jennifer Scott at Dundurn Press, an amazing Canadian enterprise that (thankfully) continues to publish my "stuff."

And while the stories that are featured in each column are mine, most of the old pictures that accompany each article, for obvious reasons, are not. To try to give credit to the individuals who took those pictures years ago would be an impossible task. Suffice to say that all of the historic images that accompany my columns have safe and secure homes in such important repositories as the Toronto Public Library, the City of Toronto Archives, the Canadian National Exhibition Archives, the Archives of the Toronto Port Authority, and the photographic collection of the *Toronto Sun*, where many of the images that appeared in the late, lamented *Telegram* can be found.

And last, but certainly not least, a heartfelt thank-you to my wife, Yarmila, for her encouragement, eagerness to help, and typing skills, and for providing three square meals a day.

Introduction

When I was a kid growing up at 758 Bathurst Street (a few giant steps south of the Bloor Street corner), I was able to see from our third-floor window the various types of streetcars that rattled up and down the busy thoroughfare. They consisted, for the most part, of the Toronto Transit Commission's (TTC's) older wooden TR cars that were built by the commission's predecessor, the Toronto Railway Company, along with a few of the TTC's 1920s-era heavyweight Peter Witt cars. With a little bit of manoeuvring in that same bay window, I was also able to watch the modern PCC (Presidents' Conference Committee) cars that quite literally glided back and forth along Bloor headed either west to the loop at Jane Street or to the Luttrell Loop out the Danforth (I have yet to figure out why it's commonly called "the Danforth" instead of Danforth Avenue).

As I got a little older (six or seven—I don't really remember), I would use my small collection of Dinky toys, a few gobs of Plasticine, and some white string and create my own streetcar routes on the linoleum floor of the back porch. Hey, I just remembered, it was from that same porch that I was able to observe the evolution of a nearby house into a huge emporium. The name of that store was Honest Ed's.

I have to believe that it was this early interest in the city's electric transportation system (buses don't count) that prompted my initial curiosity about Toronto's past.

Many years later Yarmila, my girlfriend at the time and eventual wife-to-be, bought me a gift, one of many. It was an "ancient" book entitled *Recollections and Records* and was published in 1914. It contained a compilation of author W.H. Pearson's memories of his city as it was when he was a young man. Reading this now-rare volume was something akin to smoking that first cigarette, or so I assume, as I've never smoked. I was hooked, and soon my library began to grow as I added titles such as John Ross Robertson's six-volume *Landmarks of Toronto*, a few selections from the invaluable *Goad's Atlases*, and of course the "Bible" of Toronto's architectural history, Eric Arthur's *No Mean City*.

To supplement the written words, I began searching out old photographs and souvenir postcards of the city. The former were rare, but the latter numerous, since penny postcards were the emails of the day.

One day, sometime in 1969 (the actual date is hazy, as is most of 1969 ... and 1968 ... and 1967 ...), I was contacted by Rik Davidson of the University of Toronto Press, who asked if I had ever considered putting some of my collection into book form. I hadn't but, I thought, what a fascinating idea—to have a book with my name on it. We worked quickly, and my first published work, *A Toronto Album: Glimpses of the City That Was*, hit the stores (and at least one of the national bestsellers lists) just prior to Christmas 1970. While I don't have total sales figures for my first effort, it must have been many thousands, since the book was reprinted several times. In fact, it was still popular enough that Dundurn Press, my current publisher, acquired the rights and reprinted the original in 2001. One year later Dundurn published a second volume.

Not long after my first book appeared, I had a call from the people at Toronto's *Telegram*, one of the city's newspapers back then. They asked if I would be interested in having my pictures run on an infrequent basis (what they were really saying was if and when the paper had a page it couldn't fill with an ad, they would use something of mine).

Of course, I was interested, I told them. Then I suggested running an old photo along with a contrasting modern-day view of the same scene. Initially, a *Telegram* photographer would shoot the contemporary view, but after several tries where the modern view was taken facing in the wrong direction (I guess my directions weren't totally clear and/or a copy of the old photo with all the changes in the interim was of absolutely no help), I began supplying both the "Then" and the "Now" photographs myself.

Thus began my career as a newspaper columnist. But, as fate would have it, that career, with the *Telegram* at least, was short. Months after my first contribution appeared, the 95-year-old Toronto newspaper itself became part of history when its publisher pulled the plug.

That was on Saturday, October 30, 1971. Just two days later, Monday, November 1, 1971, the *Toronto Sun* was born. Originally, the *Sun* wasn't published on Sunday, and I supplied a couple of stories during the week. Then, in the fall of 1973, the *Sunday Sun* was launched and my column began appearing in that edition. At first it was just an occasional feature, and it wasn't until sometime in early 1975 that the editors of "The Little Paper That Grew" made my "The Way We Were" column a regular *Sunday Sun* feature.

In the 30 years plus that have gone by since that first regular column in the *Sunday Sun*, there has only been one occasion when it failed to appear. And that was by no means my fault. I had taken the column into the office (in those days sending things electronically was still in the experimental stages), but unfortunately for me the newspaper had sold too much advertising for that particular Sunday edition. As a result, my column was bounced for a—wait for it!—a Crisco shortening ad. Enough said.

Since then "The Way We Were" has appeared continuously and, if I say so myself, has been well accepted, frequently being touted as one of the most popular items in the Sunday paper. I can make that statement because I am pretty sure if no one was reading it I would have been out of there a long time ago.

In 1991 it suddenly dawned on me that not everyone who was interested in my work was a *Sunday Sun* reader. Why not, I asked myself, collect some of those columns and present them to the world in book form? Kirk Howard and Tony Hawke at Dundurn Press thought the idea was a good one, and in the following year the first volume of *Toronto Sketches: The Way We Were* was published.

Thanks in great measure to Julie Kirsh, Glenna Tapscott, and Kathy Webb Nelson in the *Sun* library, who promoted the heck out of the book, the idea worked and a whole bunch of copies were sold. As a follow-up, a second volume entitled *More Toronto Sketches* appeared in 1993. That rather simple name was chosen because no one knew whether there would be any more books in what was up until then just a two-volume set.

It wasn't until a third collection of columns was ready to be presented to the public that the publisher, still Dundurn, added the number three to the title. Since then six more volumes have appeared. Now, with this special showcase of my work, Dundurn has done something truly different and unique. Happy reading ... and viewing!

1

Toronto's Passing Scene

The Toronto Girl
"Tobogganing"

Birth of a City

March 6 is a special day in the history of our city, for it was on that date in 1834 that what had been the Town of York was finally given, by royal assent, city status. (And before I get letters saying that the birth date of our community changed with the amalgamation of the city and its surrounding communities on January 1, 1998, I submit that you can only be born once.)

I describe the city as finally achieving city status because there had been several previous attempts to give the community, which had been founded by John Graves Simcoe in 1793, the ability to better administer to its needs without having to seek approval from higher levels of government. Sound familiar?

The document that made this major improvement possible had the official designation "4 William VI, Chapter 23" and was titled "An Act to extend the limits of the Town of York; to erect the said town into a city and to incorporate it under the name of the City of Toronto."

When this document was given royal assent, it resulted in the new city's boundaries being defined as: Lake Ontario to the south, Parliament and Bathurst streets on the east and west, respectively, with a line 400 yards north of Lot Street (today's Queen Street) delineating the northern boundary. Beyond the city proper would be the so-called "Liberties," an area around the new city into which the community could expand over time. The Liberties stretched as far west and north as today's Dufferin and Bloor streets, respectively, east out Lot Street to the modern MacLean Avenue, then south to Lake Ontario.

For political purposes the city was divided into five wards with two aldermen and two common councilmen representing each ward. The difference between aldermen and common councilmen had to do with the value of the property owned by their respective voters with the aldermanic position requiring higher monetary qualifications. In addition, the mayor would be elected by the aldermen from among themselves with William Lyon Mackenzie achieving the honour of becoming the city's first mayor.

And while there was a desire on the part of some of the politicians to introduce the secret ballot at the first civic election, that concept wasn't adopted until years later. In an attempt to permit the new city to be more self-sufficient the act also permitted the "levying of such moderate taxes as may be found necessary for improvements and other public purposes." Oops ... the door was opened.

One of the most controversial aspects of the act had to do with the community's name. Though the area had been known for centuries as Toronto, or some variation of that aboriginal word, it wasn't long after Simcoe arrived that he decided to honour his king back in England (and the man ultimately controlling the purse strings) by renaming the developing community after George III's second eldest son, Frederick. But rather than calling the place Frederick or some variant of that word (Freddie just wouldn't work) he selected the young prince's title, *York*, for he was the Duke of York. Thus the Town of York was born.

When it was proposed to change that name back to the original *Toronto*, there was a substantial hue and cry. Many of those opposed thought it was an affront to both the old king and his son even to consider changing the new city's name. "It must be the City of York!" they argued. Others regarded the proposed new name as being both appropriate (based on the original meaning of *Toronto* as "place of meeting") and "sonorous." Some regarded the new title of Toronto as a distinct improvement over "Nasty Little York" and "Dirty Little York" —two unfortunate nicknames the town had somehow acquired.

By a vote of 22 to 10, the Legislative Council agreed to name the new city ... Toronto.

Many Happy Returns

When "Muddy York" became Toronto that day in 1834, it was a city in name, but not much else. With a population of 9,254, it was entirely without any of the ordinary public services and conveniences recognized as essential to an urban community in our modern days. It was bounded on the south by the bay, on the east

Looking east along King Street toward Church Street in 1835, the year following Toronto's incorporation. From left to right on the north side of King are the City Jail, the Court House, and St. James' Church.

A similar view today.

by Parliament Street, on the west by Peter Street, and had a northerly limit at today's Queen Street. For the most part, the surrounding area was bush and forest.

The new city had neither water works nor sewage systems; it had no street lighting nor paved roadways. Ditches lined the streets on both sides, and in wet weather these were literally rivers of mud. And, with the exception of the tan-bark footpaths around Jesse Ketchum's home and tannery on the west side of today's Yonge Street, south of Richmond, there wasn't a sidewalk in the entire city.

Now we all know Mayor David Miller and his council have their problems to solve—the main one being fiscal in nature—and interestingly enough, the major problem faced by Toronto's first city council, led by Mayor William Lyon Mackenzie those many years ago, also revolved around financial matters. In fact, many suggested that the city not be incorporated at all because, and I quote, "the advantages of separate municipal administration would not justify the heavy additional expense that incorporation would bring." Sound familiar? If you recall, a statement made by Premier Mike Harris's government a few years ago suggested the opposite would happen with the implementation of his amalgamation proposal. In spite of all the forebodings (those of 1834, not 1997), the incorporation of the new City of Toronto went through.

However, just as today, the first city council faced money problems. The new city desperately needed to undertake a few public works projects. The first one tackled by the fledgling council was the construction of wooden sidewalks. But the materials needed to build these new sidewalks cost money. And the new city had no money. The answer? Place a tax on an individual's property with the amount to be based on ... the property's assessed value. (Ah, the dreaded "assessed value" practice, something we still grumble over.) This procedure was implemented with a tax rate amounting to "3 pence on the pound." The implementation of this "staggering" amount resulted in a public meeting being convened at the town market building. Things got out of hand and a riot ensued. So vigorously did the crowds stomp on the floors of the upper balcony that sections suddenly collapsed onto the market stalls below, resulting in the deaths of several of the protesters.

Despite the ill-fated demonstration, the tax rate remained in place. However, insufficient money was raised to construct wooden sidewalks on all of the thoroughfares, so council decided to put them only on one side of the street and only on those streets where pedestrian traffic was significant. And, in order to get as "big a bang" for the few bucks ... oops ... pounds available, it was agreed that, rather than build wide sidewalks, the 12-inch boards would be placed lengthwise; that way more streets could get sidewalks, though they would be narrower than originally hoped for.

As it turned out, getting the money for the materials was tougher than anyone imagined. That was because when the city officials approached the influential Bank of Upper Canada for a loan of £1,000 to start on the sidewalk project (to be paid back when the property tax money began arriving) they ran up against Dr. Christopher Widmer (for whom Widmer Street is named), the bank's petulant president. In the municipal election held a few weeks after the city was established, Widmer had been defeated in the race for a seat in St. David's Ward by none other than that "trivial" Mackenzie, the bane of the Family Compact's existence. Angry at his defeat, Widmer emphatically refused to loan the new city the £1,000 it had requested. As a result, the mayor and several members of his council had to go to the smaller Farmer's Bank where, after putting up personal collateral, a loan of £1,000 was approved and the sidewalks were built.

And Mayor Miller thinks he's got troubles.

Our Mother of Invention

Today, when we think of the Canadian National Exhibition, we usually think of the midway, horse and dog shows, and musical concerts at the Bandshell. But there was a time, long before shopping centres and shopping channels came into being, when what was initially called the Toronto Industrial Exhibition was *the* place to witness the latest in agricultural innovations as well as to see and try the newest of man's inventions.

Of particular interest to many fairgoers was the myriad of items that worked thanks to some new and mysterious thing called electricity. No one really knew what electricity was or how it made things work, but they could certainly get their fill of this "wonder of the age" at the Exhibition.

Interestingly, the CNE was an early proponent of electricity and has the distinction of being the first outdoor fair in the world to be illuminated at night. All those lights allowed people to stay on the grounds long after darkness had fallen. And then there was radio. In fact, the very first "plug-it-in-the-wall-outlet-and-sit-back-and-relax" variety was shown at the Exhibition in the late 1920s. These AC-powered devices, invented by young Torontonian Ted Rogers, did away with the cumbersome and expensive batteries that had been necessary to operate the now "old-fashioned" radios.

Each year the newest in refrigerators, washers, dryers, stoves, and high-fidelity and stereo sets were highlighted in the CNE's Electrical and Engineering Building, a massive structure that stood where the Direct Energy Building is today. By the way, for our younger readers, those high-fidelity and stereophonic record players your parents and grandparents saw at the Ex were the forerunners of today's MP3 players. And while on the subject of records, the oldest recorded sound in existence anywhere is the voice of Lord Stanley, Canada's sixth governor general (and yes, he was the man who donated the Stanley Cup that the Toronto Maple Leafs will one day win again). It was during Lord Stanley's visit to the 1888 edition of the fair that he recorded a message of welcome to visitors to the Exhibition from the

QUIET.....LUXURIOUS.....FAST!

See your New T.T.C. Cars at the C.N.E.

One in front of the Coliseum; one near the Dufferin Gates

Three Million Dollars spent to bring you Travel Comfort

United States. The instrument on which he made this recording was a brand-new invention from the factory of Thomas Edison, a machine that "the Wizard of Menlo Park" called the Perfected Phonograph.

Another invention witnessed for the first time anywhere in the world at the Exhibition was the trolley pole, a device still in use on all TTC streetcars by which electricity is collected from overhead wires. The original trolley pole was used on the Industrial Exhibition's experimental railway, an attraction that carried hundreds of amazed passengers on a short piece of track at the north side of the fairgrounds. They were amazed when the little cars began to move and there wasn't a horse in sight. Of course, the city's regular system used slow, plodding, horse-drawn streetcars to get people around town.

Over the next few years the Ex's experimental street railway continued to be perfected and on August 15, 1892, a similar system was put into operation on Church Street downtown. During the next two years, the entire city system was electrified using the principles pioneered at the CNE.

Other transit innovations continued to be presented to the general public at the CNE. Take for instance the introduction of the new Peter Witt streetcars by the city's newly created Toronto Transportation Commission at the 1921 fair. In 1938 a pair of PCC Streamliners—a vehicle that many claim was the best streetcar ever built—were viewed by thousands of fairgoers. In 1978 the first of the present fleet of Canadian Light Rail Vehicles was presented in Centennial Square at the west end of the grounds, and a few years later the articulated version also premiered at the Ex. And many readers will recall when a mock-up of the first subway trains also debuted at the fair ... the year? It was 1953, one year before the first section of the Yonge subway opened. Recently, two contenders in the race to replace the aging fleet of Toronto streetcars, one from Bombardier and the other from Siemens, could be viewed in front of the Direct Energy Building just inside the Princes' Gates. The tradition continues.

All aboard for the future. This experimental streetcar operated at the 1885 Toronto Industrial Exhibition.

The CNE That Was ...

There's always something new at the Canadian National Exhibition. Then again there's always something old. Take the buildings at the west end of the grounds, for instance. The cornerstone of the Medieval Times Building (originally, the British Governments Building) was tapped into place at the same time rescuers were searching for victims of the April 1912 *Titanic* sinking. By the time it opened, the nearby Horticultural Building (called by many the Flower Building) had already been a feature at the fair for five years. It sits on the site of the spectacular Crystal Palace, originally erected in 1858 near the Queen and Shaw intersection, then moved to the new fairgrounds in 1879, and finally burned to the ground in 1906.

Farther to the west we're fortunate to still have the building housing the Liberty Grand. It was built in 1926 for the Ontario government and it was here that the province told its story using state-of-the-art (for the day) live animal exhibits (I saw my first skunk there), mechanically animated displays, and, for one year at least, a huge papier mâché Paul Bunyan and his blue ox, Babe, though what they had to do with Ontario, I was never quite sure. Then, for a few years, it was the Carlsberg Pavilion, and later still, the place featured giant bugs before being turned into one of the area's pioneer casinos. When the Spanish Building burned in 1974, plans were formulated to clear away everything west of Dufferin Street. Fortunately, saner heads prevailed.

Postcard depicting the 1910 Dufferin Memorial Gate.

Even the Bandshell has an interesting history, having been dedicated in 1936, after which it became the site of the official opening ceremonies where world-famous dignitaries—premiers, governors general, lieutenant governors, mayors, war heroes ... even Bob Hope—declared the fair officially open to the roar of fireworks and the raising of a huge Canadian flag on an even more massive wooden flagpole.

Of special interest is what is now referred to as the Press Building, a delightful little structure located just north of the Princess Margaret Fountain (1958), which was originally constructed to serve as the fair's administration offices. It continued in this role until the new Queen Elizabeth Building opened across the plaza in 1957. It then became home to a variety of media representatives who covered the goings-on at the Ex for print, radio, and television. It continues in this role today while also being home to staff of the CNE Association. The building was also my home during a six-year stint as the fair's public relations and special projects manager. I loved every minute of it.

While we have retained many of the old buildings and structures, we've lost others. The postcard that accompanies this section shows one of those losses.

Postcard Perfect

The origins of the postcard in Canada can be traced back to 1871 when the federal government authorized the use of what was called a postal card. It was a picture-less, pre-stamped piece of cardboard that sold for one cent—and that price included delivery. On one side was the name and address of the recipient and on the other the message, either printed or handwritten—no pictures. In fact, the postal card was used almost exclusively by business concerns.

Next, along came the private mailing card. While one side of this type of card continued to be reserved for the recipient's name and address only, the other side could now feature

Postcard view of the sidewheeler SS *Kingston*, one of Lake Ontario's most popular passenger boats. Its usual run was from Toronto to Charlotte (Rochester), Kingston, Prescott, and the Thousand Islands.

images and, if desired, a message. It wasn't until the end of 1903 that the postcard, as we know it today, was authorized. The "divided back" card allowed the recipient's name and address as well as a message on the same side, provided one was separated from the other by a line down the middle of the card. On the other side was either an advertisement or, as this type of card became more popular, an image, often hand-tinted. The picture postcard had arrived.

Several variations of the picture postcard followed; the "white border" cards in 1914 and "linen cards" about a decade and a half later, and finally the "chromes," a glossy-surfaced postcard, typical of those that tourists purchase today. By the way,

The Armouries on the east side of University Avenue, north of Queen Street, was erected in the early 1890s. After a spirited battle of its own, the old structure was demolished in 1963 to make way for the University Avenue Court House that now sits on the site.

the term *chrome* originated with the 1939 introduction by Kodak of its Kodachrome film.

Accompanying this section are postcards depicting a downtown street scene, a popular passenger lake boat, and a prominent city building. These subjects were typical of the images found on the "divided back" cards in circulation by the thousands throughout the country after 1903.

This postcard view looks north on Yonge Street to the Carlton Street intersection circa 1915. A little farther to the north was the College Street corner. These two cross-town thoroughfares weren't joined, as they are today, until the spring of 1931.

Torn from the Headlines

One of the great things about writing a column about Toronto's history is that every so often readers will send along items that are related in some way to our city's history. Usually, these items consist of old postcards or family photos with an old building in the background or a street scene with lots of what are now regarded as "collector" cars zipping in and out of traffic. However, one day I received something out of the ordinary. It was the front page of the February 20, 1865, edition of *The Leader*, an "ancient" Toronto newspaper. I can only assume that the person who sent it along didn't appreciate its historical value because it was literally torn from the rest of the paper—I don't even want to think of what happened to the other pages.

The Leader began publishing on July 1, 1852, as a twice-weekly newspaper. It was printed in a small shop at 9 Leader Lane at the northwest corner of Colborne Street—the site is now occupied by part of today's King Edward Hotel. It was the presence of *The Leader* office that resulted in the small street on the east side of the hotel being called Leader Lane, a name it still retains. On July 7, 1852, *The Leader* began publishing on a weekly basis, and it eventually became a daily on July 11, 1853. The last edition was published in 1878.

One feature of the old newspaper clipping was its condition, for even after 140 years it was almost as legible as it was when it first came off the press. That's because the paper on which it was printed consisted of refined cotton or linen fibres obtained primarily from rags. With no harsh chemicals used in the process, my old paper will remain pliable for many years to come. Conversely, today's newspapers become fragile as a result of chemicals used to give the paper its brightness—over time, chemical residue reacts with the atmosphere causing the paper to turn yellow and brittle.

Some of the items carried on the front page of *The Leader* included business listings for a number of barristers—a few of the surnames are familiar today as Toronto street names: Gamble, Boulton, Osler, and Blevins. There was a "Traveling Directory" with an ad for an omnibus that left the Yonge and King corner seven times a day for what was described as the "north eastern" parts of the county, and another offering to sell six acres of land in Yorkville, "a portion of which is presently leased for $60 annually." Dr. Hallick, whose office was at 159 Church Street, was offering to permanently cure something called "seminal weakness." The good doctor could also be consulted confidentially for every complaint of the "organs of generation." News

stories included one on the "Oil Region of Canada West" that had been carried in a recent edition of the *New York Times*. The American news story described the product being pumped to the surface (from the Oil Springs area of Ontario) as being "more substantial in combustion and furnishes a brighter light" than that found in Pennsylvania. The report went on to indicate that while the volume of oil is huge, there are too few uses to which it can be put.

Sharp-eyed readers will have noticed that this edition of *The Leader* appeared just a couple of months prior to the end of the American Civil War. With this in mind, one of the ads on the front page is especially intriguing. Under the heading "Friends of Federal Soldiers," an anonymous entrepreneur offers to arrange for local families to communicate with "prisoners of war in the south" by placing a notice in *The Leader*—at a charge of up to four lines for a dollar. Copies of the paper would then be sent to Richmond, Virginia (via Halifax), in hopes that the person being sought would somehow be alerted to the notice. Any reply would be placed in Richmond's *Enquirer*, copies of which would be sent (again via Halifax) to Toronto.

Water Tanks ... for the Memories

Instead of identifying the pictures that accompany this section, I'm going to ask you two questions about them. The first is: what prominent Toronto intersections are depicted in each of these old photographs? I'll give you the answers at the end of the section. And the second question, what once-prominent feature of the Toronto skyline of years past can be seen in all three of these photos? Look closely. Give up?

Visible in the photos are elevated water tanks. They represent just a couple of the dozens of similar tanks that could be found all over town early in the last century. To be sure, there are a few elevated water tanks that continue in service (the one at Mr. Christie's bakery on Lake Shore Boulevard West near the Humber River comes to mind). In addition, the City of Toronto still has four mammoth water storage tanks. The two that I immediately think of (since I frequently drive by them) are northeast of the Leslie and Lawrence intersection and southeast of the corner of Eglinton and Warden.

Prior to the introduction of modern, efficient, and reliable mechanical water storage tanks—usually fabricated out of steel with a few of the older types made of wood (usually clear-cut redwood or cypress)—were recognized as the best way to ensure that a building had a sufficient supply of water, under pressure, for either sanitary or process use inside the building or as a source of a huge quantity of water in the event fire erupted within the building.

Before the introduction of standby electrical generators, it wasn't unusual for a power failure to disrupt the flow of water, thereby forcing businesses to shut down until power could be restored. In fact, it was the failure of the city pumping system to maintain sufficient pressure in the hydrants that resulted in the uncontrolled spread of flames that destroyed much of downtown Toronto in mid-April 1904. Owners of several buildings in the path of the fire, including that housing the presses of the *Telegram* newspaper at Bay and Melinda, were able to minimize damage to their structures through the use of water curtains fed by rooftop water storage tanks.

Now, as to the identification of the photos accompanying this section, the one above (bottom) looks south on Bathurst Street toward Front and was taken in July 1917. The streetcar is crossing the former 1903 railway bridge that spanned the Humber River at its

FILEY *Fact*

Although now deemed an "essential service," there was a time when members of the Toronto Police Department did go on strike. The date was December 18, 1918, and the cause of the unrest was the Board of Police Commissioners' decision to fire 11 members of the force who attempted to organize a union that would be affiliated with the Trades and Labour Congress of Canada. Once unionized, the police could go out on strike. The strike lasted three and a half days. A royal commission was established to look into the grievances.

mouth. When a new, stronger bridge was needed to replace the old structure at the foot of Bathurst, the city decided to save money and purchased and recycled the old Humber Bridge. The road's deflection to the west was eliminated in 1931 when Bathurst was straightened out down to the newly constructed Lake Shore Boulevard. That resulted in the demolition of the Matthews and Blackwell meat processing plant along with its elevated water tank seen in among the trees to the left of the bridge.

The photo on page 38 looks north on Spadina Avenue over King Street. While the specific date is unknown, the cars would indicate the photo was taken sometime in the late 1920s or early 1930s. Obvious in the view are the two elevated water tanks, one serving the W.G. Gage factory at 82–94 Spadina Avenue, the other atop the nine-storey Darling Building just up the street at 86–104. Interestingly, Gage was in the wholesale books and stationery business and, while at its previous location on the north side of Front Street West between Bay and Yonge, had been burned out in the 1904 fire. The rooftop water tank seemed like good insurance against that happening again.

The photo on page 39 (top) looks north on York Street across Front in 1925. The billboards and old building in the background would be levelled the following year when work began on the new Royal York Hotel. The water tank to the extreme right is on top of one of the old factory buildings on the west side of Bay Street, north of Front.

On the Beat Since 1834

It was January 1, 1957, that what we now know as Toronto Police Service came into being—the result of a long-debated plan to amalgamate the 13 different police departments that up until then had patrolled the streets of the Municipality of Metropolitan Toronto. Originally, the Metropolitan Toronto Police Department, that name was changed to the present Toronto Police Service coincident with the "birth" of the new City of Toronto in 1998.

As the Toronto Police Service enters its second half-century of service to its public, policing in Toronto actually has a history stretching back to 1834, the year the Town of York relinquished that title and became the City of Toronto. The population was 9,254, and to keep an eye on things, the city fathers, under Mayor William Lyon Mackenzie, hired William Higgins as Toronto's one and only paid police officer. If and when things got out of hand, High Constable Higgins had the authority to call on as many civilian volunteers as he felt necessary to assist him in restoring order. It wasn't until the following year that the city approved the hiring of five full-time paid officers. Two years later, in 1837, officers were issued regulation uniforms, forest green in colour. Records of the era indicate that these policemen spent much of their time catching and reprimanding shopkeepers who threw their garbage on the street. Seems our city has always prided itself on clean streets.

An important change in the administration of the police occurred in 1859 when control was turned over to a Board of Police Commissioners rather than leaving it in the hands of municipal politicians. The board included a county judge, the local police magistrate, and the mayor, Sir Adam Wilson. This distinguished gentleman was the first mayor in the city's history to be elected, not by council members as was the custom of the day, but by the voting public.

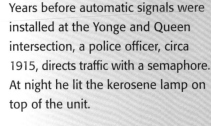

Years before automatic signals were installed at the Yonge and Queen intersection, a police officer, circa 1915, directs traffic with a semaphore. At night he lit the kerosene lamp on top of the unit.

Over the ensuing years the city's police department continued to implement the latest technological advances to try to stay one step ahead of the criminal element. For instance, in 1874, police stations were linked by telegraph. Call boxes to permit communication with officers on the beat were installed at designated street locations in 1887. And it wasn't long after the new-fangled safety bicycle made its North American appearance in the late 1880s that officers

The Toronto Police Mounted Unit was established in 1886. In this undated photo an officer is seen patrolling in High Park.

were using them to expand their patrol areas. In doing so, Toronto became the first police department on the continent to use bicycles to fight crime. The Mounted Unit was established in 1886, motorcycles were added to the fleet in 1911, and patrol cars rolled into use just 11 years later. And while one would think that parking tickets came after the department added the motorized equipment, in fact, the first of those ubiquitous tickets had been issued in 1907. In 1909 the police department was given the responsibility of regulating "traffic, parades, and processions."

Other Toronto Police Department firsts include: 1913, the first policewoman; 1925, the first electrically controlled traffic signal (at Yonge and Bloor); 1935, the first in-car radios (one-way dispatcher to car); and 1953, the first use of radar to enforce speed limits.

While the police department serving the citizens of Toronto was evolving, so, too, were the other 12 police departments serving the smaller communities that surrounded the big city—Etobicoke, Mimico, New Toronto, Long Branch, North York, Scarborough, East York, Leaside, York, Weston, Swansea, and Forest Hill. With the creation of the Municipality of Metropolitan Toronto in 1953, an action that placed some of the responsibilities formerly looked after by the individual civic governments under one new authority, Metro Toronto, discussions on what to do with the separate but intertwined police departments began. It took some time, but on January 1, 1957, the new Metropolitan Toronto Police Department came into being under former Toronto Police Chief John Chisholm. With the creation of the new City of Toronto in 1998, the department was again modified and now operates under the title of Toronto Police Service.

FILEY Fact

There are more than 2,000 electronic traffic control signals scattered throughout the city. The very first method of traffic control at busy intersections was to assign a police officer who would use a manual "stop and go" traffic semaphore. The first electronic device was erected at the Yonge and Bloor intersection in August 1925. Unlike today's vertical traffic lights, the four installed at this corner were positioned horizontally.

Grab Your Easter Bonnet

One of the longest-running traditions in Toronto is the celebration of Easter with a parade. Some of these parades are religious in nature while others celebrate the arrival of the Easter Bunny and the longer, warmer days that accompany him/her. The parade in the Beach part of town is an example of the latter.

Unlike the parades of today, a key element of the Easter parades of yesteryear was the opportunity they afforded to preview for the public one's new spring outfit. In fact, some of the earliest photographs taken in and around our city show smartly dressed Easter crowds promenading along the wooden sidewalk adjacent to the dirt-covered Lake Shore Road that skirted the old Humber Bay. A popular complement to the afternoon's outing might be a visit to Pauline Meyers's restaurant, located right on the water's edge and visible in the background of the old photo. In addition to her tasty fish dinners, Pauline had an interesting hobby. When requested by the family, she would make a brooch containing strands of hair from the deceased individual. Such "mourning jewellery" had become popular following the death of Prince Albert in 1861 and Queen Victoria's decision to wear a piece of jewellery that incorporated a lock of her dead consort's hair.

Strolling along the old Sunnyside boardwalk, circa 1907.

Soon after the new Toronto Harbour Commission was created in 1911, plans for the redevelopment of the city's waterfront, from the Humber River on the west to Victoria Park on the east, began to take shape. One area that would undergo a massive change was the old Humber Bay and the area around it. The water would be filled in and a new park and highway along the water's edge created. The highway would evolve into the western section of today's Lake Shore Boulevard—the initial plans called for it to cross the Western Channel and skirt Toronto Island, connecting with the mainland again at Cherry Beach. The park would become Sunnyside Amusement Park, which came complete with rides, games, dance halls, and restaurants. Opening in the spring of 1922, the park quickly became the new home of the city's annual Easter Parade. For the next 33 years, thousands made their way to Sunnyside to show off their new outfits.

When the park closed in the fall of 1955, the parade was on the move again, this time to Bloor Street between Yonge Street and Avenue Road, where on several occasions the sidewalk was painted in pastel colours to harmonize with many of the new spring outfits. Traffic and modern times eventually put an end to the Bloor Street parade. In the early 1960s, a new Easter Parade, under the sponsorship of the Beaches Lions Club, took over Queen Street East, where it continues bigger and better than ever.

Celebrations in History

Happy Dominion Day! Oops ... I mean Happy Canada Day! Oh, well, it was an honest mistake, since that was what the July 1 holiday was called for most of my young life. In fact, the term *Dominion Day* was used from 1879—a dozen years after Confederation—until October 27 of 1982 when the federal government decreed the annual holiday would henceforth be known as Canada Day.

Back when the holiday was still called Dominion Day, many people spent the day at Sunnyside, the city's most popular amusement park. Located on Toronto's western waterfront near the foot of Roncesvalles Avenue, the park was a magical place that came complete with rides, games, fast-food stands, a huge swimming tank, and dance halls. The park opened in 1922 and was a favourite for Torontonians and visitors to the city until something called "progress" forced its closure following the 1955 season. Today only the Sunnyside–Gus Ryder Pool and newly restored Palais Royale remind us of a gentler, simpler time.

As popular as Sunnyside was, it certainly wasn't the city's only amusement park. In fact, there were three out on Queen Street in the Beach (note I said "beach," singular) area of the city, and while all of them disappeared years ago, all three are remembered in names of east end city streets.

The oldest of the three parks was Victoria Park. In fact, it was just over the city boundary in Scarborough Township and was developed in 1878 on a portion of the country estate of one Peter Paterson, a retreat he called Blantyre, the source of one local street name. In addition to picnic grounds, the heavily treed site had donkey rides, several carousels, a shooting gallery, and other attractions. Initially, access to the park was only by water, specifically the steamer *F.B. Maxwell*. Before long the pioneer Toronto & Scarborough Electric Railway opened a new single-track line that made it easier for people to get to the park by streetcar. Victoria Park lasted another few years before the amusements were dismantled and the grounds turned over to the city's Board of Education as the site of one of its two forest schools. It was believed that these schools—there was another in High Park—would allow a child's "mental, moral, and physical development to be enhanced by prolonged contact with the natural environment." The Victoria Park forest school was closed when the city began clearing the site prior to starting construction of the sprawling R.C. Harris Water Filtration Plant. Today the only reminder of this popular amusement park can be found in the name of the concession road that ran north from the property— Victoria Park Avenue.

A second amusement park in the same general vicinity opened in 1896. It was named Munro Park to honour—though somehow it was spelled incorrectly—the original property owner, George Monro. Incidentally, this was the same George Monro who served on Toronto's first council in 1834 and also had a one-year term in 1841 as the city's sixth mayor. This park had a dance pavilion, Ferris wheel, merry-go-round, and, for a period of time, an exhibit of live ostriches. Munro Park was closed in 1907 when land in this area of the city became more valuable for housing lots. Today's Munro Park Avenue is a reminder of that old amusement park and, coincidentally, one of the city's pioneer politicians.

The most successful of the three parks out on Queen Street East was Scarboro (that's the way it was spelled) Beach Park, an immensely popular place that opened more than 100 years ago. The park would be located on what had formerly been a farm operated by the Sisters of St. Joseph. The produce grown on this farm fed the unfortunates residing in the House of Providence, located on Power Street in downtown Toronto. A private syndicate eventually purchased the property and in 1907 opened a $600,000 amusement park modelled after a similar enterprise on Coney Island.

SPECIAL CAR SERVICE
FROM
Queen and Yonge Sts.
DIRECT TO
SCARBORO BEACH
Every Evening from 7 p.m.
and SATURDAY AFTERNOON

Making transfer connections with cars at Queen and Yonge Sts. and Richmond and Yonge Sts.

Scarboro Beach Park was one of three amusement parks located on Queen Street East in the Beach area of Toronto. Pictured here is one of the park's many popular rides, circa 1910.

In 1913 the Toronto Railway Company, the city's street railway operator, took over the park and ran it as a "trolley park." Common in many American cities, trolley parks allowed companies to use vehicles that would otherwise be simply stored in the car barns to carry crowds of fun-seekers to and from the park during summer evenings and weekends.

In 1925 Scarboro Beach Park was offered to the city's new publicly owned streetcar company, the TTC. But the TTC said "no thanks" and the park closed following the 1925 season. Within a couple of years the park's scenic railway, lacrosse stadium, shoot-the-chutes, and sideshows had been replaced by houses and sidewalks with Scarboro Beach Boulevard bisecting the site.

History of Improvement

Numerous civic improvement projects have been carried out during Toronto's 175-year history. One of the first such undertakings was the laying of wooden sidewalks along one side of King Street in the newly established city's downtown shopping area near the St. Lawrence Market. However, a shortage of money (sound familiar?) meant that to get the maximum distance out of the few wood planks the city of some 10,000 citizens could afford to purchase, officials were forced to have them placed lengthwise rather than in the more conventional crosswise fashion.

As the city grew, other amenities became necessary to ensure a clean, livable city. It took time, but eventually a reliable supply of clean water was in place, sewers and storm drains were laid, sewage treatment facilities were built, roads were paved, splintering wooden sidewalks were replaced by concrete walkways, and a regular garbage pickup schedule was established (although we're still struggling with what to do with the stuff once it's been collected).

Other major civic improvements followed, such as a massive cross-waterfront railway viaduct to serve the city's new Union Station, the building of a mile-long traffic artery spanning the valley of the Don River (thereby opening the eastern part of the city to development), the creation of an efficient public transportation system, and the establishment of a modern flying field at Hanlan's Point with a backup facility out in the countryside near the farming community of Malton. The

FILEY Fact

The disposal of the thousands of tons of garbage generated each year in the City of Toronto has become a major topic of discussion. Years ago the solution was simple: collect it, burn it, and use what was left as landfill. Many hollows and ravines throughout the city were removed through the use of this residue. This method was a step up from the original winter disposal method that consisted of carting the waste material to the bay, dumping it on the ice, and letting the warmer weather look after the problem.

list of municipally sponsored improvements is lengthy, but there was one highly touted civic improvement that many felt was nothing more than a tremendous "boondoggle." Known as the Don Improvement, this project, which was given provincial approval on March 26, 1886, would see the river confined to a 120-foot-wide, 14-foot-deep channel from the Winchester Street Bridge—that was located south of today's soaring Prince Edward Viaduct—to its new confluence with Toronto Bay. In addition, an 80-foot-wide strip of new land would be created on either side of the channel on which a rail line and roadway would be laid.

Straightening the Don would accomplish several things. First, it would eliminate the swamps that existed adjacent to the meandering river. These swamps had been the breeding grounds for mosquitoes that had led to frequent outbreaks of malaria and were considered one of the reasons the young city grew in a westerly direction away from the river. In addition, some businessmen believed that with the river in a wide, deep channel, ships that plied the Great Lakes would be able to make their way up the river to new docking facilities that would be erected as far north as the Queen Street Bridge. These new docks would in turn prompt the construction of nearby factories that in turn would be served by railways that would lay their tracks on the reclaimed land. All in all, there was no doubt that the Don Improvement would lead to tremendous industrial growth for this part of the city that had for so long been overshadowed by the growth in industry and business west of Yonge Street.

Looking north up the Don River from the Wilton (Dundas) Street Bridge, March 27, 1916. Ice frequently caused problems such as this. In the distance is the Gerrard Street Bridge with the Don Jail on the horizon to the right of centre. (City of Toronto Archives)

History tells us that while the mosquitoes may have been routed and the river straightened, the proposed

Similar view today. A different camera lens makes the "new" Gerrard Street Bridge appear closer. The section of the Don Valley Parkway seen here (Gardiner Expressway to Bloor Street) opened in 1964.

improvements resulting from that straightening never materialized and no large freighter ever ventured up the Don River.

There was, however, another form of transportation that did gain something as a result of the Don Improvement project. Initially, the plan called for railway tracks to be laid on the newly reclaimed land on either side of the straightened river. These tracks would connect with the sidings built to serve the new factories that would surely be erected in anticipation of the lake freighters being able to ascend the Don River channel. One set of tracks was owned by the Canadian Pacific Railway, which for years had been trying to obtain a direct route into the heart of the bustling city, only to be thwarted time after time. Somehow, during the process of straightening the river, the CPR managed to extend its rail corridor along the west bank of the river right through to the city's old Union Station and waterfront freight yards. The Grand Trunk (later the CNR) also obtained a rail corridor; it's located on the east bank of the river. With the construction of the Don Valley Parkway in the early 1960s, the lines were combined in a corridor on the west side of the lower Don and are still used by GO Transit and freight trains today.

The second set of bells for Toronto's St. James' Cathedral are stored on Toronto Street awaiting installation in the church's newly constructed spire. The original set was lost in a shipping accident on the St. Lawrence River.

The Bells, the Bells

It was on Christmas Eve 1865 that the nine bells in the steeple of St. James' Cathedral rang for the first time. Interestingly, those bells weren't the original ones that church officials had purchased for the cathedral. The originals were lost when the ship transporting them from England, where they had been cast, sank in the St. Lawrence River. Another set was quickly ordered from the Meneely Foundry in Troy, New York, and these are the bells Torontonians heard for the very first time that Christmas Eve long ago, and are still heard (though there are now 10, with a large brass bell added in 1925) throughout the neighbourhood as they peal each quarter-hour.

Supplementing the Meneely bells is a set of 12 "change ringing" bells. They were installed in the cathedral's tower and dedicated on June 27, 1997, in celebration of the establishment of St. James' first congregation exactly 200 years earlier when St. James' was still known simply as the church at York.

Unlike the older set of bells that are rung mechanically using a keyboard, the change ringing bells, known as the "Bells of Old York," are rung by volunteer bell ringers. Eight of these bells originally hung in the tower of St. James' Church, Bermondsey, located in East London, England. Deemed unsafe in the deteriorating tower where they had been installed in 1829, the bells were purchased and shipped to Toronto. The London church then used the money from the sale of the old bells to strengthen the tower in which eight lighter-weight bells were installed.

Back in Toronto, it was decided that St. James' would purchase four additional bells from the Whitechapel foundry where the Bermondsey bells had been cast more than 150 years before. In doing so, St. James' Cathedral would have a peal of 12 bells, one of the largest such complements on the continent. All of the money raised for this endeavour, approximately $500,000, came from the general public. No cathedral funds were used for the project.

Ring in the New Year

On January 17, 1900, city officials took delivery of the clock that was to be installed in the soaring tower of the city's new $2.5 million municipal building at the top of Bay Street. Work on the building, the one we know today as "Old" City Hall, had actually started more than 10 years earlier. Tired of work slowdowns and stoppages, on September 18, 1899, a very impatient chief magistrate Mayor John Shaw demanded that, ready or not, the unfinished building be opened for business. As it happened, two of the new hall's most

This photo, taken in 1899, shows Toronto's new and as yet unfinished "Old" City Hall waiting for its clock and bells to be installed.

notable features that weren't ready in time for the opening were its huge tower clock and the associated trio of bells, two "Ting Tang" quarter-hour bells weighing 1,907 pounds and 2,915 pounds respectively and the mammoth 11,984-pound hour bell.

Interestingly, the invoice for this equipment, a copy of which I obtained some time ago from the manufacturer—Gillett & Johnston of Croydon, England—reveals that the order wasn't signed until September 13, 1899, a mere six days prior to the mayor's forced opening of his new City Hall.

As of yet, I have been unable to find out why the order was so late in being placed. This lateness, however, accounts for the fact that the clock and related pieces such as, as the order states, "escapement, pendulum, wheels, pinions, pulleys, connecting rods, arbours and a quartet of 20-inch-diameter Illuminated Dials," didn't arrive in Toronto until 16 months after the then new City Hall opened.

Several more weeks passed before the trio of bells arrived from the same factory and were placed in position. They rang for the first time at midnight, January 1, 1901, to welcome the arrival of the new twentieth century.

Calling 1947!

They're everywhere! They're everywhere!

Older people have them, teenagers have them. Heck, even little kids have them. In fact, information supplied by the Canadian Wireless Telecommunications Association informs us that there are more than 19 million subscribers using these things across Canada, a nation with an estimated population of just over 33 million.

And just what are these things I'm talking about? Cell phones, that's what. And based on the figures supplied by the CWTA I've just quoted, there's a good chance that when you're next sitting in the car at a traffic light, the drivers in the vehicles on either side of you will be on the phone. And who knows? The way things are going (the CWTA reports that cell phones are among the fastest growing consumer products in history), most of those without a cell phone might just have one come Tuesday.

The cell phone phenomenon all started more than 60 years ago with a series of experiments with the goal of establishing wireless communication using what were initially called mobile radio-telephones. And some of those tests were conducted right here in our city by the Bell Telephone Company of Canada. Their experiments went like this.

First, a radio transmitting station with a range of 20 miles was set up on the top floor of the Bell Building at 76 Adelaide Street West. In addition, several of the company's green-and-black sedans were outfitted with low-power receiving and sending sets and were conspicuous with 18-inch antennae on the roof. These vehicles would then wander the city to establish where signals between the car and the radio station worked best.

It wasn't long before it became obvious that the 20-mile range of the main station was insufficient to cover the sprawling (even back then) city. The numerous tall buildings in the downtown core also interfered with the signals. To get around these problems, "repeater stations" would have to be established at various locations across the city where special equipment would capture the signals and send them on to the Bell Building on Adelaide Street via the regular telephone lines.

Each of these locations would soon be known as a "cell." Thus it was that over time the original term *mobile radio-telephone* was replaced by the term *cellular phone* and eventually shortened once again to the modern-day *cell phone*.

But I'm jumping ahead of myself. In those early days, placing a "mobile call" to and from a vehicle was no easy task. It required the assistance of a special Bell operator.

Let's say that the boss sitting in his office wants to contact an employee out on a delivery somewhere. A call is made over a regular phone to the "mobile operator" who then sends out a radio signal on a channel that's specifically for that vehicle. That signal causes an audible or visual warning in the car telling the driver he's being paged. The driver then picks up the in-car phone to begin the conversation, having first set the equipment to "receive" to hear the boss's request, then to "talk" to tell the boss just what he could do with that request. That same driver could also call home from the car, but the steps to do so were slightly different. Picking up the mobile phone in the car, he would push the "talk" button and the mobile operator would respond and be given the driver's home phone number. The call would then be placed by the operator. Once the home phone was answered,

George Curtis, an engineer with the Bell Telephone Company of Canada, is seen testing one of the company's experimental car telephones in early 1947.

the conversation would take place again using the "talk" and "receive" buttons, though this time requests made by the wife would usually be carried out without additional comments.

Although the mobile service got off to a slow start, by 1953 Toronto's *Telegram* newspaper was reporting that the mobile telephone network was serving vehicles on the streets and highways in the Toronto and Barrie areas as well as in and around Montreal.

Bell's wireless phone service, housed in Molson Brewery's mobile rescue trailer, turned out to be invaluable during the rescue operations that followed the Hurricane Hazel disaster in mid-October 1954. And now there are BlackBerrys and iPhones. What next?

Mayor Foster's Care

Once, in one of my columns, I described how Thomas Foster, who served as mayor of Toronto in 1925, 1926, and 1927 (back then, municipal elections were held annually), had arranged to spend eternity with his wife, Elizabeth, and daughter, Ruby (both of whom had predeceased him). He had a mausoleum designed in the Byzantine style which, as Foster often commented, was inspired by the famous Taj Mahal in India that he had visited following his retirement from the political scene.

Foster selected as the site for this mausoleum a plot of land a few miles north of the

The real Taj Mahal in Agra, India.

town of Uxbridge. It was near here that he had spent his childhood before he moved to the City of Toronto. With the financial horrors brought on by the Great Depression still very much in evidence, the local newspaper found Foster's idea of building a $200,000 "grave" perfect material to fill their pages. Stories began to appear from the moment work began on its design and subsequent construction through to the dedication ceremony on October 25, 1935—performed by Foster himself.

With the dedication out of the way, a little more than a decade went by before Foster was again in the newspapers. This time, though, they were writing about his death, which took place on December 10, 1945, at his rather ordinary-looking residence on Victor Avenue in the Riverdale area of the city. There was also a summary of this fascinating Torontonian's long life. It read in part:

Mourners attend Thomas Foster's funeral, which was held at his unique mausoleum on December 13, 1945.

> *Following Foster's from Uxbridge to Toronto, the young man purchased a meat market on Queen Street East near Berkeley for $50. He always spent the profits from his business wisely and almost always on real estate. Before long, he was worth a fortune. He decided to enter the world of municipal politics in 1891, was successful, and over the next 36 years served as alderman, controller, and finally as mayor of the city. In fact, many said it was his frugality with the taxpayers' money that had won him three successive terms as the city's chief magistrate. But as frugal as Foster was with spending money from the city's treasury, he frequently, and anonymously, helped ordinary citizens in financial difficulty with money from his own pocket. Also unknown to most people was the fact that Foster's real estate investments had made him rich. Following his death his estate was valued at more than $1 million.*

Interestingly, almost all the money Foster made during his lifetime would, under the terms of his last will and testament, be given back to his city and its citizens. In the preamble to his will, Foster advised he was doing so "to mark my appreciation of my citizenship in Toronto, and to place in the way of some citizens or their children opportunities for health and advancement which might not otherwise be theirs."

While no one is sure about the cause of death of either his daughter, who died at age 10, or his wife, who passed away while still a young woman, there may be clues in two of his largest bequeaths. He left $600,000 for cancer research and another $25,000 for the maintenance of special wards for tuberculosis victims.

Other lesser amounts were set aside to fund an annual children's picnic (an event that continues to be held) and to help beautify the city through the planting of trees and shrubs along the highways leading to Toronto. Money was also earmarked for the purchase of bird seed. The Foster estate also funded two flagpoles, "specifically of Canadian timber," that were to be erected in front of Central Technical School and in front of Toronto (Old) City Hall.

The former mayor also directed that $10,000 be used to purchase movie projectors and radios for the entertainment of patients in the Hospital for Incurables in Parkdale. He further requested that $5,000 be divided among 10 of that hospital's patients who had no other source of income "to be spent as they may, in their own absolute discretion." Other amounts went to a variety of churches, including $500 to the Salvation Army for the maintenance of instruments of the Riverdale Corps' Silver Band.

Certainly, the most controversial of Thomas Foster's bequests was his desire to financially assist women who had many children. He directed money to be awarded to moms who had lived in Toronto for at least a year and who had given birth "in lawful wedlock" to the largest number of children in each of four 10-year periods. Those with the largest number in each period would receive $1,250, the second largest $800, and the third largest $450.

Thomas Foster (1852–1945).

2

Toronto's War Years

UNIVERSITY AVENUE, TORONTO

Days of Defeat

This breaking news just in! Even as thousands of Americas are celebrating the nation's centennial, news has arrived that Civil War veteran turned Indian fighter Colonel George Armstrong Custer along with 262 members of the U.S. Cavalry's 7th Regiment have been killed near the Little Big Horn River in the Montana Territory during a bloody two-hour battle with Sioux and Cheyenne Indians under Chief Sitting Bull. At this very minute our crews are on their way to the site of one of the worst military defeats in American history. We'll have an update on the situation as soon as possible!

Lieutenant William Winer Cooke, Colonel George Custer's second-in-command at the Battle of the Little Big Horn, June 25, 1876.

The above might have been how the world would have learned about the now-famous (or is it infamous) "Last Stand" by Custer had CNN, CBC, CTV News, or even the *Toronto Sun* been in business back in 1876. But, of course, they weren't. Many days would pass before the true and almost unbelievable extent and humiliation associated with Custer's defeat became known.

Over the decades that have passed since, the story of the battle has been told in numerous books, in a variety of television programs, and in several major Hollywood motion pictures. Was Custer a true hero or an egotistical fanatic who simply wanted to wipe out the Native Americans who he perceived as his country's enemy? More than 130 years later, find two people and you'll get two opposing answers.

There was something of particular interest to Canadians when the news of the battle finally appeared in the local papers on July 7, 1876. Many readers recognized the name of Custer's second-in-command on that fateful day. And it was of special significance to those living in the "Ambitious City" of Hamilton, Ontario.

William Winer Cooke was born on May 29, 1846, in the village of Mount Pleasant, a small community not far from Brantford, Ontario. As a young man, he attended both Brantford Collegiate and Hamilton's Central School. At the age of 14 he moved to Buffalo, New York, to continue his studies. The following year saw the outbreak of the American Civil War, and though he wasn't yet 18—he told the recruiting sergeant he was 22—Cooke joined the 24th Regiment, New York Cavalry. In 1864 he became an officer in the 9th Union Army Corps under General Burnside—whose unique facial hairstyle gave rise to the word *sideburns*. The terrible war finally over, Cooke was mustered out and soon returned to Canada. But the tranquility north of the border didn't sit well with Cooke, and when he learned that his friend from the Civil War days, George Armstrong Custer, had been appointed second-in-command of the newly organized 7th Regiment of U.S. Cavalry, it wasn't long before the young Canadian was back at his friend's side with the rank of second lieutenant. On several occasions Custer visited Hamilton where he met his young lieutenant and stayed with the Cooke family in their Walnut and Main Street residence.

Details are scarce on just how the 30-year-old Cooke met his fate at the Little Big Horn. We do know from a small piece of paper on display at the library of the West Point Military Academy that it was Cooke who sent Trooper Martin for help when things looked bleak for Custer and his men. The note reads "Benteen [Captain F.W. Benteen, commanding Troop "F"]. Come on. Big Village. Come on. Be Quick. Bring (ammunition) packs. P.S. Bring Packs" and was signed W.W. Cooke.

William Winer Cooke was buried, along with Custer and all the troopers who died at the Little Big Horn that remarkable day years ago, at the scene of the battle. Some years later Cooke's remains were brought home and interred in Section CC-B, Lot 63, of the Hamilton Cemetery on Plains Road.

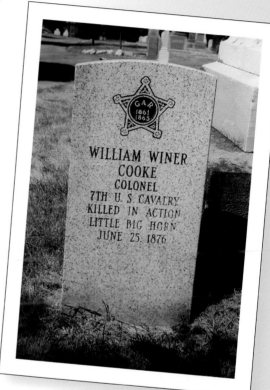

Lieutenant Cooke's final resting place in the Hamilton cemetery.

Path to a Great Tribute

While Remembrance Day services are held at numerous sites around Ontario every year, one of the most enduring is the ceremony staged every November 11 at the Cenotaph in front of Toronto's Old City Hall.

Interestingly, the first Remembrance service held in front of Old City Hall didn't occur until November 11, 1920, the second anniversary of the end of the Great War. On that occasion an estimated 10,000 people gathered in front of a makeshift Cenotaph. Two minutes of silence were observed, but not at 11:00 a.m., as we do today, but at noon.

The previous year, 1919, there was no official Remembrance Day service in front of the Municipal Building. In fact, the newspapers reported that on that day when the bells in the City Hall tower struck 11:00 a.m. those attending meetings in the Municipal Building observed two minutes of silence, then went back to work. As for the staff in City Hall, a flicking on and off of the building's interior lights was followed by two minutes of silence. Around the downtown core that day, many simply stopped what they were doing at 11:00 a.m. and stood with heads bowed for two minutes. One of the streetcar motormen even brought his packed vehicle to a halt right in the middle of the busy King and Yonge intersection, then removed his cap and waited until the two minutes had passed. Others quickly recognized what was happening and did likewise. Not a horn or a disgruntled voice could be heard where seconds before the noise of a busy city filled the air. No sooner had the traffic returned to normal than great quantities of ticker tape floated down from the open windows of the nearby CPR Building, just as it had exactly one year before when word was received that "the war to end all wars" was over.

Many might think that the very first Remembrance Day would take place on the same day that the armistice was signed, that is, November 11, 1918. However, as people began to learn that war was finally over—the news had actually arrived by wire at 2:30 a.m.—most were far too excited to think about anything other than that it was time to celebrate. The streets soon filled with cheering crowds while the various outlying neighbourhoods began decorating homes with red, white, and blue bunting. Bonfires were set and business ground to a halt. It was party time!

Soon the true horror of what had taken place over the past four years began to sink in. In particular, the thought that, of the 60,000 Torontonians who had left to fight "for king and country," 10,000 would never return. This quickly put a damper on the festivities. The mood had changed and, in keeping with the sadness that began sweeping the city, Mayor Church declared that Sunday, November 17, would be observed throughout Toronto as a Day of Thanksgiving. Perhaps this was the city's first true Remembrance Day.

Initially, the citizens honoured their fallen by placing wreaths around a makeshift Cenotaph—a word that means "empty tomb"—in front of City Hall. It wasn't until late 1924 that the city fathers agreed that a permanent one should be erected. The task of designing a proper Cenotaph was awarded to the Toronto architectural firm of Ferguson and Pomphrey, with the actual work being done by the McIntosh Granite Company at its yard on Yonge Street, next to the CPR station (now a beautiful LCBO store). The design chosen was a smaller version of the Great Cenotaph at Whitehall in London, England. The cornerstone was tapped into place by Field Marshal Earl Haig on July 24, 1925, and the completed monument was unveiled by Governor General Baron Byng of Vimy the following Remembrance Day.

A permanent Cenotaph was erected in front of what was then Toronto City Hall (now Old City Hall) in 1925. Up until then a temporary monument was used. This view was taken shortly after the new Cenotaph's official unveiling by Lord Byng, Canada's governor general, on November 11 of that year. Note the old buildings on the south side of Queen Street and the TTC's Peter Witt streetcars.

Prior to the unveiling, a small controversy arose over the wording on the monument. Originally, those words read "To those who served." After being reminded by more than a few citizens that a Cenotaph was literally an "empty tomb," city officials ordered those words replaced by "To our glorious dead."

In Praise of Our Heroes

Thousands gather each year at Canada's National War Memorial in France to pay their respects to those Canadians who either risked their lives or made the supreme sacrifice during the Great War. The location of this memorial is on a high ridge not far from the community of Vimy. It was here, over a four-day period more than 90 years ago, that Canadian forces did what no other Allied units could—dislodged huge numbers of German troops from a position the enemy had held for more than two years.

During those two years, the Germans had turned the ridge into a fortress from which they were able to decimate the British, French, and other Allied troops clustered below. It was obvious the ridge had to be taken at all costs. So the Allied generals eventually agreed that the Canadian Corps would be assigned what heretofore had been an impossible task: they were ordered to take Vimy Ridge.

Plans to ensure that the battle would succeed were immediately undertaken, and

The memorial to Canada's fallen at Vimy Ridge in France, designed by Toronto's Walter Allward, was picked from 160 entries submitted from around the world. (Library and Archives Canada)

on April 9, 1917, the battle began. Four long days would pass before the Canadians could claim victory. The fierce fighting for Vimy Ridge resulted in more than 10,600 Canadian casualties. Of that number nearly 3,600 were killed.

Once the successful capture of Vimy Ridge was achieved, the Canadians went on to distinguish themselves in many more battles. But it would be the victory at Vimy Ridge that would become legendary.

In 1920, nearly two years after the end of the First World War, the newly established Canadian Battlefields Memorial Commission organized a competition to select designs for Canadian memorials to be erected on each of eight battle sites—three in France and five in Belgium. One of those sites was to be near Vimy, and the person selected to design its memorial was Walter Seymour Allward.

Allward was born in Toronto in 1875 and lived on Seaton Street. He attended the nearby Lord Dufferin School on Parliament Street for a short time before obtaining employment at the brick works in the Don Valley. Allward took painting courses but much preferred sculpting, and eventually moved into a place on Walker Avenue where he built himself a small studio. It was here that he worked on his first "real" commission, one that we can still admire today. Unveiled in 1895, the North-West Rebellion Monument is located on the west side of the Ontario Parliament Buildings.

Several other commissions followed before Allward was given the opportunity to create a grand memorial to those Canadians who fought and lost their lives in the South African War (1899–1902). This major piece of work, which still soars over the University Avenue and Queen Street West intersection, was unveiled on May 24, 1910.

Toronto's Walter Allward (1876–1955), creator of the Vimy Ridge Memorial.

Over the next few years, Allward completed other projects. However, when he learned that a memorial was being sought for the Vimy battlefield site in France, this project became a priority. Allward prepared more than 100 designs but chose to submit only one. Of the 160 ideas submitted from all corners of the British Empire, Allward's was the winner.

Upon receiving the news, Allward moved into a studio in London, England, where he began the preliminary work on the massive project. Actual construction on the ridge began in 1925 and was to continue for 11 years. Interestingly, one of Allward's inventions, one that allowed carvers to transform his small half-size plaster models into the 20 giant limestone figures that grace the monument, was a device he had created while working on the South African War Memorial in downtown Toronto.

The spectacular Vimy Ridge Memorial was unveiled on July 26, 1936, by King Edward VIII. In 1996 it was designated a National Historic Site, and eight years later the Canadian government initiated a program that would see the structure restored and maintained in a manner that respects the historical and cultural integrity of Walter Allward's original design.

It's Over, Over There

May 8 marks the anniversary of Victory in Europe Day, or VE Day, as it quickly became known. While historically May 8, 1945, marks the end of the war on the European continent, the nearly six-year-long conflict actually seemed to stagger to an end. Early in the month there were continuing rumours suggesting the war would be over momentarily. Those rumours grew stronger each day and finally on Monday, May 7, and even though the official announcement hadn't been made yet, many Torontonians jumped the gun. A day that had begun as the start to just another work week quickly deteriorated into a day of sheer pandemonium.

Crowds celebrate VE Day on Yonge Street. (City of Toronto Archives)

Impromptu parades began to take shape all over the place, usually led by someone with a Union Jack and another reveller with a drum or trumpet. Over at the corner of King and Yonge, celebrating citizens were kept busy dodging the wooden spools attached to the ends of long rolls of paper that came hurtling down from the city's office buildings.

Up in Queen's Park, an effigy of Herr Hitler that someone had secretly created and hidden made an appearance and was quickly put to the torch. Back downtown, the Toronto Stock Exchange opened as usual, but within a half-hour all trading was curtailed, traders being unable to complete the transactions with all the festivities taking place on the trading floor of the Bay Street building. At Osgoode Hall, and other law courts throughout the city, officials told those waiting to have their cases heard to come back another day.

Overhead the unmistakable drone of several recently completed Mosquitoes from the de Havilland plant in North York Township could be heard as they buzzed the town in a victory fly-past. Farther to the west, the pilot of a small Fleet trainer from the Leavens Brothers flying school on Dufferin Street just north of Lawrence Avenue flew over downtown, throwing red, white, and blue steamers from the open cockpit.

It seemed that the only place where calm prevailed was at the University of Toronto where students were writing—and continued to write—their final exams. As the joyous news continued to spread, most of the city's businesses started to shut down so their employees could join the festivities. Not to be left out of all the fun, a quick-thinking railway official dispatched a special train to collect the war workers out at the Victory Aircraft factory near the airport and bring them downtown to join in the celebrations. It was at the Victory plant that the giant Lancaster bomber, so important to the defeat of the Axis powers, was still rolling off the assembly lines.

The Toronto-built Lancaster bomber pictured in this 1999 photo on display south of the CNE grounds is currently being restored at the Toronto Aerospace Museum in Downsview Park.

Among the many places that closed were the majority of downtown restaurants. That resulted in both the Active Service Canteen on Adelaide Street East as well as the IODE canteen being overwhelmed by servicemen and members of the public who were seeking something to eat or a hot cup of coffee or tea.

It was Monday, May 7, 1945, and Torontonians were going crazy.

The next day, Tuesday, May 8, a day U.S. President Harry Truman had officially declared as "Victory in Europe Day," would be quite a contrast. The realization that thousands of Canadians would never return home, quickly turned a rejoicing city into one that began reflecting on the losses it had suffered.

VE Day in Toronto saw the city's many churches crowded with worshippers while several of the larger city parks hosted open-air services of thanksgiving. Everyone realized that, while the war in Europe had indeed ended, the conflict in the Pacific was still very much a concern. There would be more tears and sorrow.

An Anniversary of Note

August 15 marks the anniversary of another important event. It was the date the world celebrated the end of the war in the Pacific. It was at noon, Japan Standard Time, that Emperor Hirohito addressed his nation, via a phonograph recording played over the radio, that his country had accepted the terms of the Potsdam Declaration—interestingly, the word *surrender* was never used in the emperor's speech to his people. The actual date for celebrating VJ Day varies, with the United States adopting August 14 as the day, since that was the date the news broke across American time zones.

In Toronto the acting mayor of the day, David Balfour—a long-serving city father for whom the park in the Mount Pleasant–St. Clair part of town is named— was even more confused. With the devastation of both Hiroshima and Nagasaki, the free world was sure the end of the war was imminent. In fact, so certain was Prime Minister William Lyon Mackenzie King that peace had arrived that he went on the radio on Sunday, August 12, and announced in no uncertain terms that the war was over. When told of King's announcement, Balfour quickly proclaimed the next day a public holiday. Oops! Once the prime minister's gaffe was confirmed, poor Mr. Acting Mayor had to retract his offer of a Monday holiday.

Nevertheless, when it finally became official, VJ Day in Toronto was treated in a similar fashion to the VE Day events three months earlier. On Tuesday, August 14, street parties spontaneously erupted all over the city, and while long lines of citizens paraded through all the downtown streets, there was no more joyous place than Toronto's Chinatown—for reasons that will be obvious to anyone who has studied the early stages of the Pacific war. As with the VE Day celebrations three months earlier, the day of the announcement was filled with rejoicing. That was followed on the Wednesday by a day of solemnity, with churches and synagogues crowded to overflowing. Services of thanksgiving were held in various city parks. One of the largest such events filled Kew Beach Park in the city's east end with an estimated 10,000 happy but reflective, citizens.

While on the subject of the Second World War, I once received a note from Ted Barris, a faithful reader of my newspaper column and author of *Days of Victory: Canadians Remember 1939–1945*, who wondered if anyone could help him track down "Ronnie, the Bren Gun Girl." In his letter, Ted related that "During the war, thousands of Canadian women left so-called traditional work stations—in homes and offices—and assumed jobs in munitions factories across the country.

Ronnie the Bren Gun Girl became Canada's version of the American icon Rosie the Riveter. (Library and Archives Canada)

They went to work building tanks, planes, and weaponry so that men could be free to join the nation's armed services. So powerful was this phenomenon that Veronica Foster, who worked at assembling Bren guns at the John Inglis plant on Strachan Avenue, became a national icon when she was featured on a wartime poster. Veronica soon became Canada's version of the Americans' 'Rosie the Riveter.'" More than that, Ronnie Foster represented a social movement in this country. According to wartime journalist Lotta Dempsey, women in war work represented "the honest-to-goodness equality of Canadian women and men in all the work of this country."

Toronto Pleasure Palaces

Kicking Up Our Heels

Often, when I'm asked to speak to groups about the history of our great city, one of the topics that comes up over and over again relates to the various dance halls that many in the audience remember visiting when they were younger. I will focus here on a few of the better-known ones. At the top of that list would certainly be the Palace Pier. Jutting into Lake Ontario at the mouth of the Humber River, the Pier was a favourite place to gather to dance to many of the American big bands as well as to some of the best that Canada had to offer, including those led by Ellis McLintock and Trump Davidson. Interestingly, the Palace Pier was also known as the Queensway Ballroom, which must have been confusing, since The Queensway was well to the north, across the railway tracks.

Next in a very long list of Toronto dance halls would be the Palais Royale, located on the south side of Lake Shore Boulevard and originally a major attraction in old Sunnyside Amusement Park. The Palais was recently restored to its former glory (and not a minute too soon). The regular band at the Palais was Bert Niosi and His Orchestra. While we're visiting Sunnyside, there was a place nearby that was just as popular as the Palais, provided it was warm and not raining. The Seabreeze was *the* place in town for those who wanted to dance under the stars. It disappeared in the fall of 1955 along with the rest of the park and another dance hall, the Club Top Hat (formerly the Club Esquire), located across Lake Shore at the Parkside corner.

The Top Hat, formerly the Esquire, in its heyday on Lake Shore Boulevard.

Over on the Toronto Islands there was the Pavilion at Hanlan's Point where Paul Firman's Band could be heard when he wasn't playing at the Masonic Temple at Yonge and Davenport (now a TV studio). Moving uptown, there was the St. Regis Hotel (Jimmy Amaro and

His Orchestra) and Columbus Hall (Jack Evans, who was often heard during the summer at the Seabreeze), with both places located on Sherbourne Street.

On Bloor Street West, at Belair, was the remarkable Club Embassy. Described as a "high class restaurant and dancing club," the place was organized by a syndicate made up of 17 members of the city's elite. It was to be the most sophisticated of its kind in the country and was to be run along the lines of the Embassy Club, Bond Street, London, England. The club opened in late 1928 and unfortunately, with only $4.63 in the bank, had to declare bankruptcy a little more than a year after it opened its doors. Seems Toronto wasn't as "worldly" as many thought. It reopened some years later but without the pizzazz the backers envisioned.

About the same time the original Club Embassy was getting organized, Sir Henry's Pellatt's former residence on the hill, under its entrepreneurial and innovative new manager William Sparling, was in the process of introducing the public to dancing at Casa Loma. It was Sparling who brought Jean Goldkette's Orange Blossoms to town from Detroit. In 1933 the band, now led by Glen Gray (who played saxophone under his real name Glen Gray "Spike" Knoblaugh in the original band), changed its name to Glen Gray and the Casa Loma Orchestra. The group was featured at the castle for the next eight months. The stage had been set, and over the following years orchestras led by Mart Kenney, Benny Louis, Paul Grosney, and Art Hallman filled the Great Hall with the sounds of the big bands.

The Palais Royale Reborn

With all the talk these days about the revitalization of Toronto's waterfront, especially the area east of Yonge Street, another project, this time well to the west of Yonge, is quietly reviving one of the city's few remaining landmarks from the days of the big bands.

Walter Dean was a master boat builder who ran a small factory on the Humber Bay shoreline at the south end of Parkdale. His beautiful Sunnyside Torpedo canoes were known far and wide. When the Toronto Harbour Commission began to implement its 1911 plan to revitalize Toronto's western waterfront (see, revitalizing the waterfront isn't a new idea), Mr. Dean had to move until the work of filling in the old Humber Bay was complete.

He set up shop for a time near the foot of York Street, then in 1921 returned to the Harbour Commission's newly created waterfront out Sunnyside way where

The Palais Royale during its salad days.

PARK PLAN DANCING—10c A DANCE
GRAND OPENING OF THE NEW
Palais Royale Ballroom
Saturday Night
Featuring
Harry Bedlington Orch. and Belva White
NO COVER OR ADMISSION CHARGE

he constructed a new building in which to continue building his canoes. To supplement his boat-building business, he also operated a small restaurant on the main floor where dances were occasionally held. Dean's business failed in 1922, the same year the adjacent Sunnyside Amusement Park opened. It was then that a new company called Palais Royale Limited took over the building and continued to operate the place as both a restaurant and a boat livery.

In 1928 the company tried to turn the place into a high-class supper club. But that didn't work and for a time the building, now known to most Torontonians as the Palais Royale, was boarded up. Then, in 1932, a pair of amusement park concessionaires, Bill Cuthbert and George Deller, reopened the place as a dance hall. The dance band they hired was Harry Beddlington and His Whispering Orchestra. Admission was 25 cents plus a charge of 10 cents a dance. But with money being tight (the Depression, you know) the place was just too expensive. Again the Palais was in trouble.

Into the picture stepped Joe Broderick, who brought with him one of the city's most popular bands—one that he just happened to be managing. The combination of Bert Niosi and His Orchestra, a reduced 10 cent admission, and a nickel-a-dance policy quickly turned things around. Then Broderick decided to try something new, at least for Torontonians. He brought one of the biggest of all the American dance bands to the Palais, and on an early September evening in 1933, Eddie Duchin and His Park Central Orchestra filled the place to overflowing with nearly 3,000 fans. The Palais Royale became *the* place in town to hear and dance to the big bands.

In the years that followed, virtually all the name bands from south of the border made the trip north to the Palais. Some of the busiest times at the Palais Royale were those of the Second World War, with servicemen and women eager to celebrate before going overseas. But with the end of the war came changing habits, the closing of the amusement park, television sets, and the Gardiner Expressway—soon the Palais Royale was seen as an out-of-the-way place with no future. The question was: what would come first, planned demolition or premeditated fire? As it turned out, however, a trio of young entrepreneurs stepped in and, with special regard for the old dance hall's historic past, the Palais Royale was brought back to life.

Casino Royale

Downtown Toronto is filled with splendid theatres. Among them are the Princess of Wales, the Royal Alexandra, the Canon, the Elgin and Winter Garden, Massey Hall, the Sony Centre (formerly the Hummingbird Centre), and the St. Lawrence Centre. As popular as these places are, they are probably no more exciting for today's theatre-goers than was the old Casino for Torontonians of yesteryear. This old theatre was located on the south side of Queen Street, a few steps west of Bay and opposite the future site of the city's long-planned-for New City

Toronto's popular Casino Theatre, Queen Street West, opposite the future site of New City Hall. The movie being shown, *The Preview Murder*, was released in 1936, the same year the Casino opened.

Hall. In fact, it was this latter structure, now over 40 years old and yet still referred to as "new," that was the primary reason the Casino was finally demolished. It had no place in a modern downtown Toronto.

Built in 1936 in the art deco style, the Casino had seating for 1,200 patrons and, as some said, perfect acoustics. Two years after it opened the place came under the management of Lou Appleby and Murray Little. The two first met when Lou's father, who owned the Roxy Theatre a few doors east, was killed in his upstairs office while counting the day's receipts; the murder remains an unsolved case.

Initially, the Casino featured a program of burlesque acts complete with some sort of striptease performance followed by a third-run feature film. However, in the early 1950s the theatre's focus changed, and soon American performers on their way up the ladder of success began sharpening their talents in front of appreciative Canadian audiences. The list of those who played the Casino a half-century ago can only be described as amazing. Here are the names of just a few: Tony Bennett, Peggy Lee, Eartha Kitt, Pearl Bailey, Mickey Rooney, Victor Borge, Patti Page, The Mills Brothers, Tommy Dorsey, Mel Tormé, Canada's Oscar Peterson, Van Johnson, Vaughn Monroe, Marty Robbins, Henny Youngman, Dorothy Lamour, Jane Powell, Basil Rathbone, Gene Nelson, Ella Fitzgerald, The Ames Brothers, Louis Armstrong, Hank Snow, Helen Forrest, Cab Calloway, Les Paul and Mary Ford, Duke Ellington, Eddie Fisher, Rosemary Clooney, Julius La Rosa, The Platters, The Andrew Sisters, and Al Martino. The largest crowds in the theatre's

FILEY *Fact*

Over the years Toronto has had dozens and dozens of movie houses, ranging from small neighbourhood theatres to magnificent 2,000-seat picture palaces. And it all started in 1906 when John Griffin opened his Theatorium on the east side of Yonge Street just north of Queen Street. The place was nothing more than an empty store with wooden planks for seats and a white rectangle painted on the wall that served as the screen.

history came in the spring of 1953 to see "Mr. Emotion" himself, pop-singing star Johnny Ray. And it was at the Casino that Toronto's own Four Lads started out on their road to stardom.

As plans began to unfold for the new city hall across Queen Street, the Casino attempted desperately to stay with the times. In 1962, as the Civic Square Playhouse, it tried presenting legitimate theatre. Two years later it was renamed again, and this time, as the Festival Theatre, offered international films. Nothing seemed to work and, in 1965, the old Casino, along with the other old buildings in the block (including Henry's Cameras that resurfaced over on Church Street), was expropriated and soon demolished.

The Sheraton Centre now stands on the site where thousands of Torontonians were entertained by dozens of entertainers who went on to become show business icons.

Coulda Danced All Night

I have written about some of the many places where an older generation of Torontonians could go dancing—the Palace Pier, the Palais Royale, Club Top Hat, Seabreeze, Columbus Hall, and the St. Regis Hotel. Here are a few more of the lesser-known dance halls, the location of each, and the name of the house band.

Player's Hall at the southeast corner of Broadview and Danforth, where Alf Hannigan and the boys often appeared, was popular with the people in the east end of the city, while those living in the west end found the Arcade at 101 Roncesvalles Avenue the place to be. At the latter, for only a dollar, a couple could dance all night to the music of Bas Cheeseman and His Orchestra.

An unusual dance hall was located at 1001 Dundas Street West. It was known as Liberty Hall and was described by newspaper ads as the place where every Friday night there were dance and swing sessions for anyone who was a jazz fan. But rather than live music, this place played new American and imported records (remember those?) that featured such musicians as "Slam" Stewart, "Flip" Phillips, and the King Cole Trio. As an added extra, visitors could pay to have any of the records they heard and liked re-recorded so they could take the music home. I wonder if that was legal back then.

Farther north, the Wexford Arena, on Dawes Road (now Victoria Park Avenue) near Sheppard Avenue, also featured Friday night dancing, this time to the music of Billy Hole and His Live Wires. Over in Swansea, the Silver Slipper, on the west side of Riverside Drive just north of The Queensway and backing onto the Humber River, presented Mickey McDougall and His Orchestra playing what management called "a distinctive style of dance music" every night of the week—except, of course, Sunday. After all, this *was* Toronto. The only difference between the six evenings was that admission was only 50 cents per person Monday through Thursday, with that figure bumped to 75 cents on Friday and Saturday. The Slipper also boasted "the largest and most modern dance floor in Canada" as well as "new and efficient dining room service." Unfortunately, the Silver Slipper burned to the ground in early 1958. A gas station now stands on the site.

Here are a few more places people went to dance back in the "olden days." On Lakeshore Road just over the Humber was the Hollywood Hotel where dancers could swing to the music of The Ambassadors (featuring Ruth Cameron, "the little lady of song") or Len Davis and His Band. On Cowan Avenue just south of Queen was the Masaryk Ballroom where The Acadians as well as Dr. Fred Evis and His Orchestra were featured throughout the week. On Saturday night the popular Stan Porch Orchestra took over. Up near Woodbridge, Mart Kenney's Ranch opened its doors to dancers (couples only, please) on June 24, 1949. The popular Stampede Room was added two years later. Way out in the east end of the city, not far from the junction of Danforth Avenue and Kingston Road, was the White Castle Inn. The featured band there was Jack Currie's. Not far away, at Stop 31 on Kingston Road, was Club 31 where Dick Walker and His Band played for your dancing pleasure.

Of course, most of the city's bigger hotels, the Barclay (Front and Simcoe), Prince George (King and York), the King Edward, and the Royal York, also had dancing, but they were more expensive and usually saved for those extra-special occasions.

The Play's the Thing

It was a special day in the nation's theatrical history when Toronto's very own Royal Alexandra Theatre turned 100. The theatre's origins go back to a time when little wooden streetcars were the rapid transit vehicles of the day, today's "Old" City Hall was *the* City Hall, and a blackberry was simply a summertime treat. The new theatre's opening more than 100 years ago was celebrated with all the pomp and ceremony that the fast-growing city of 275,000 souls could muster. Lieutenant Governor Mortimer Clark was there, as was a beaming Mayor Emerson Coatsworth, and they were surrounded by a crowd made up of the city's elite.

The playhouse was built by a consortium consisting of some of Toronto's wealthiest gentlemen led by Cawthra Mulock, Canada's youngest millionaire and a representative of one of the city's most influential families. Cawthra was born in 1884 and was educated at Upper Canada College and the University of Toronto. At just 15 years old he was the beneficiary of a huge $3 million inheritance from his great aunt, Mrs. Cawthra-Murray, and by the time he had reached the age of majority that amount had more than doubled. He invested wisely and was soon a very rich man. However, Cawthra was continually troubled by the fact that many of his business contacts overseas knew nothing about the young man's hometown. In an effort to change this lack of knowledge, the young man brought together a few of his partners—including stockbroker R.A. Smith, manufacturer Stephen Haas, and entrepreneur Lawrence "Lol" Solman—and together they built what was soon regarded as "one of the finest playhouses on the North American continent," an accolade the Royal Alexandra retains to this day. Sadly, Cawthra died at the age of 34, another victim of the Spanish influenza epidemic.

The site chosen for the Royal Alexandra Theatre was originally occupied by old Upper Canada College. The school, which was established in 1829, relocated to Deer Park in 1891.

The architect of the new theatre was John Lyle, who just a few years later would participate in the designing of Toronto's new Union Station on Front Street. The Royal Alexandra Theatre, which was named after the wife of the reigning monarch King Edward VII (who in turn is honoured in the name of the King Edward Hotel just along the street), was constructed on the former playing grounds of Upper

Canada College, a long-time Toronto institution that had only recently moved north to the "wilds" of Deer Park and a forested countryside location not far from today's busy Avenue Road and St. Clair intersection.

The work chosen to open the new $750,000 playhouse was entitled *Top of the World* and was described by the PR flacks of the day as a "pantomime extravaganza." It had a cast of nearly 100 and was an instant hit, allowing management to hold the show over for two weeks and charge a lofty $2 per patron for the best seats in the house.

As the years passed, the theatre began showing its age and its future became more and more uncertain. Then, in 1963, in a move that surprised everyone, Toronto businessman Edwin Mirvish came to the rescue. "Honest Ed," who most Torontonians simply knew as the proprietor of a discount store at the corner of Bloor and Bathurst streets, purchased the sadly wilting theatre for $215,000. He then proceeded to spend another $350,000 to restore and rejuvenate the Royal Alex to a condition it hadn't seen since it opened in 1907.

Under Honest Ed's regime the theatre was used primarily for touring shows and pre-Broadway tryouts. It also saw productions by local performing arts organizations such as the Canadian Opera Company and the National Ballet of Canada. The extremely popular satirical revue *Spring Thaw* was also a feature of the Royal Alexandra. Two homegrown productions, *Hair* in 1970 and *Godspell* two years later, were presented at the Royal Alex and were noteworthy successes.

In 1975 the theatre was protected under the Ontario Heritage Act. A dozen years later the Royal Alexandra was declared a National Historic Site.

On the Sunnyside

When we hear various government departments announce imminent changes to Toronto's waterfront, many people may think such proclamations are new. While specific projects may be innovative, the idea of altering the waterfront in various ways certainly isn't. In fact, it was as far back as 1927 that the citizens of Toronto were told of a planned $1.25 million development that, should it be approved by the Toronto Harbour commissioners and sufficient funds raised from the public to undertake its construction, would change the look of the city's western waterfront forever. The proposed project would be known as the Sunnyside Palace Pier and would be similar to the amusement piers scattered all along the coastline in England.

But the Provincial Improvement Corporation, an English company with local offices in the Northern Ontario Building at the northwest corner of Bay and Adelaide streets, promised that Toronto's new pier would be much more impressive than its namesake attraction in Brighton, England. At a projected cost of $1.25 million it would also be far more costly to build.

The financial prospectus that was given to potential investors described the new Sunnyside Palace Pier as consisting of four structures: a 30,000-square-foot ballroom that would accommodate 3,000 couples, a huge "Palace of Fun" that would include a roller rink (converted for ice skating in the winter months), a large outdoor Band Pavilion seating 1,500 in hammock chairs, and a luxuriously appointed 1,400-seat theatre. There would also be 39 concession buildings in the form of restaurants, souvenir stores, and the like. All these structures would sit atop a gaily illuminated pier stretching nearly a third of a mile out into Lake Ontario from the Etobicoke Township side of the mouth of the Humber River.

There would even be provisions for lake steamers from near and far to tie up along the pier, allowing thousands easy access to this, as the prospectus pointed out, "the greatest of all-year-round amusement enterprises." The document went on to describe the project as catering to the tourists and amusement seekers alike with a daily projected attendance in the range of 50,000 people.

The promoters hoped to finance the project by the public sale of $10 shares in what they described as a "can't lose" proposition. The money began to flow in slowly, and it wasn't until early January 1931 that the cornerstone of the first building was tapped into place by Arthur Meighen, the former Canadian prime minister. But, as with many projects of the era, financial difficulties, not the least of which was the onset of the Great Depression, would intervene. Soon the money needed to complete the entire project dried up, resulting in only a few hundred feet of pier ever being built.

And even when this part of the project was completed, the abbreviated pier stood empty for years. Finally, on June 23, 1941, the Strathcona Palace Pier roller skating rink opened to the

public. Several days later radio and movie star Bob Hope, who was in town promoting his latest film, *Caught in the Draft*, christened the new Palace Pier by doing a few laps around its shiny hardwood floor.

Over the years the old pier was home to a variety of public events. It was the perfect venue for the American big bands, with virtually every organization but that of the legendary Glenn Miller (actually Miller appeared only once in Toronto and that was at the Mutual Street Arena in 1942) appearing at the Queensway Ballroom as the pier was renamed.

As the big band craze died out (though Ellis McLintock and His Orchestra held on for a time), the place became home to a variety of other public events, including boxing and wrestling matches, religious revival meetings, country and western concerts, and high school proms.

It all ended early in the morning of January 7, 1963, when an arsonist set the historic building aflame. A towering condominium now occupies the site. At the southwest corner of the property there is a display of pictures and artifacts of the original Palace Pier.

Flames could be seen as far away as Hamilton and St. Catharines as fire destroyed Toronto's famous Palace Pier.

The Gardens

It was on the evening of November 12, 1931, that 13,542 enthusiastic hockey fans paid anywhere from 95 cents to $2.75 to watch the first event to be held in the city's brand-new Maple Leaf Gardens. And it was only right that the mammoth new facility should open with a Toronto Maple Leafs hockey game. And while the home team lost that special game to the Chicago Black Hawks 2–1, what really mattered was that their beloved Maple Leafs had a hockey palace that was among the finest anywhere.

The idea of building a new facility to replace the old, outdated Mutual Street Arena where the Toronto team had played both as the St. Patricks and, after February 15, 1927, as the Maple Leafs, was a business decision, pure and simple. With a seating capacity of only 8,000, the Arena was making it more and more difficult for team owner Connie Smythe to come up with enough money to cover the ever-increasing salary demands of the better players in the NHL. Smythe was convinced that a larger building with more seats would mean extra money—money that could be spent on superior players and a better chance at winning Lord Stanley's coveted trophy.

Even though the world's financial markets were collapsing all around him, Smythe, with help from some of Toronto's most influential businessmen, was able to obtain sufficient backing to get the project started—on paper at least. But even before all the money was in place the first decision that would have to be made was exactly where to locate the new arena. Smythe had his eye on a large parcel of land near the corner of today's Yonge and Lake Shore Boulevard, not far from the Air Canada Centre, the Gardens' eventual replacement and the Leafs' home rink since February 20, 1999.

Unfortunately for Smythe, the land in question was unavailable for outright purchase and Smythe wanted no part of any leasing arrangement. So he continued his search, and before long property owned by the T. Eaton Company on the north corner of the Yonge-College-Carlton intersection came on the market. However, Smythe preferred another of the Eaton properties, the one at the northwest corner of Church and Carlton—just steps from both the busy Carlton and Yonge streetcar lines. This site was perfect.

After considerable negotiation, Eaton's not only consented to sell the property but agreed to purchase $25,000 worth of stock in Smythe's new venture, as well. The next step in getting the Gardens built involved finding additional sums of money in the midst of the ever-worsening financial depression. When a deal was reached that resulted in most of the workers taking stock in lieu of real dollars, Smythe's dream of a new hockey arena began to look more and more promising.

Finally, work began in March 1931 with the demolition of a number of dilapidated stores and houses on the Eaton property. Construction of the new Gardens started in earnest on June 1, 1931, and in less than six months, Smythe's new Maple Leaf Gardens was ready for the first puck to be dropped. A little trivia—that puck was dropped by William Stewart, the Toronto mayor at that time.

Unfortunately, the hometown boys lost that opening game to Chicago. But take heart, dear fans. Even with that disappointing start, the team went on to win the Stanley Cup that season.

By the way, I see that dedicated Leafs fans have recently been able to watch some of the team's away games in high definition at a number of local movie houses. I was sure this wasn't the first time hockey games were presented at a theatre, and

Newspaper ad for the February 21, 1965, Toronto Maple Leafs–Detroit Red Wings hockey game to be shown on the big screen at seven local movie houses.

I was right. During a chat with former CITY-TV personality Lieutenant Governor David Onley recently, we both recalled seeing Leafs games through the magic of Eidophor, a Swiss invention that permitted the projection of closed-circuit TV signals onto large screens such as those found in several Toronto movie theatres. Famous Players, a company that had suffered serious setbacks with the coming of home television in the early 1950s, installed a number of Eidophor projectors in their theatres and began showing sporting events such as boxing matches and hockey games. The first Maple Leafs game to be seen on the movie screen was the one between Toronto and Chicago that opened the 1962 season. The place selected to pioneer what was described as "a new kind of Sports Entertainment" was the College Theatre at College and Dovercourt in west-central Toronto, admission $1.25 to $2.50 with "Smoking Permitted in Loge Seats."

Records indicate that watching Leafs games on large screens at local movie houses ended in the mid-1960s. Now they're back.

The more things change the more they stay the same.

4

Toronto at Work

More Power For Ontario

Hydro's Richard L. Hearn Generating Station goes into operation at Toronto

A Hit, One Tire at a Time

Readers who drive through the Lake Shore Boulevard East and Leslie Street intersection will no doubt have noticed the new Canadian Tire Store at the southwest corner. Others may remember the building it replaced—a gargantuan Brewers' Retail warehouse. This sparkling new building is a far cry from the dilapidated old garage on Gerrard Street East opposite the Don Jail where the story of Canadian Tire began in 1922.

It was in that year that the Billes brothers, John and Alfred, took a chance and, pooling their meagre resources, purchased a small automobile servicing business that operated under the rather grand title of Hamilton Tire and Rubber (in reality it was small neighbourhood garage at the southeast corner of Gerrard and Hamilton streets). The venture set the boys back exactly $1,800.

John and Alfred were in business for just a short time when the city decided to do major repairs to Gerrard Street and the nearby bridge over the Don River. The construction chaos had a major impact on the boys' business and they nearly went bankrupt.

It was then that John and Alfred decided to move into the city proper, and the following year they opened a shop at the corner of Yonge and Gould streets in downtown Toronto. They stayed in this location for two years, and in 1925 moved nine city blocks north into what at some point in its long history had been a grand old residence at the northeast corner of Yonge and Isabella.

Business was good, with more and more orders arriving daily from across the nation for the company's brand of tires and batteries. Business was so good, in fact, that the Billes brothers agreed that Hamilton Tire and Rubber needed a change of

Located at the northeast corner of Yonge and Isabella streets, this old building was Canadian Tire's home from 1925 to 1930. The structure still stands and is now the home of House of Lords Hair Design.

name: Now with hundreds of customers all across Canada, what better name could there be than Canadian Tire?

As business increased, more space was found in a larger building at the southeast corner of the intersection. This was followed by a move farther north to a site most readers will no doubt remember, especially if I remind them that some of the staff wore roller skates to get around the sprawling store more swiftly.

FILEY *Fact*

In January 1946, an ad appeared in Toronto newspapers advising customers that a brand-new product was now available at Simpson's department store—one that "would do that paint job in a fraction of the time." The advertisement continued, "This improved paint roller has a water- and rust-proof cylinder [and] the roller runs on free-running bearings with the 'Koter' [the roller portion] interchangeable and useable with all types of paint."

The ad showed a sketch of something called the "Koton Koter." It was actually part of a set that also included what appears to be a wooden tray. Both items were available for $1.98, with replacement rollers just 69 cents each.

About the only other thing we know about Breakey's "Koton Koter" is that it's rumoured that the prototype and some early models were assembled in an old building that still stands at the southeast corner of Dupont Street and Westmoreland Avenue in west-central Toronto.

THE NEW
"Koton Koter" Set
1.98

This building, located on the east side of Yonge just north of the Yonge-Church-Davenport intersection, had only recently been constructed as a produce market to serve the citizens of North Toronto. For whatever reason, the market idea didn't work out and, in the fall of 1936, the Billes brothers bought it and moved in. While the old building still stands, Canadian Tire now operates out of a new building just to the north of it that was constructed a few years ago.

Today Canadian Tire operates more than 460 stores across the nation and serves nearly three million customers each week. The Billes boys would be pleased.

Banking on Canada

In 1855 a group of prominent businessmen representing one of the most important enterprises in Canada West (to be renamed Ontario in 1867), the grinding and milling of grain, met in Toronto to create a new financial institution to provide banking and insurance support as well as provisions for commodity exchange that were specific to their unique form of business. After much discussion, the new bank was born, and in honour of its birthplace it was called the Bank of Toronto.

The bank grew and prospered, and in 1860 it opened a branch in Montreal, the first to be established outside its home province. Seven years later the new Dominion

Before the arrival of the new Toronto-Dominion Centre in the mid-1960s, the Royal York Hotel (left) and the Bank of Commerce dominated the city skyline.

of Canada came into being. With an optimistic eye toward the infant nation's future, several industrialists and financiers obtained a federal charter for another financial institution, and in 1871 the Dominion Bank of Canada came into being.

Over the years—and despite two world wars and what was termed the Great Depression—both banks continued to serve their customers and the nation. Then, in 1954, officials of the two institutions agreed that amalgamation would be advantageous on all levels. So, on February 1, 1955, the Toronto-Dominion Bank, with 449 branches and a combined staff of nearly 5,000 employees, was born.

Less than a decade later, the Toronto-Dominion Bank decided to create a complex of buildings that would not only transform the heart of a city where the original two banks first entered business but would place Toronto on the world's banking stage. The first tower of the now six-tower Toronto-Dominion Centre was officially opened by Ontario Premier John Robarts on May 14, 1968. The special significance of the TD Centre was recognized with an Ontario Heritage Foundation plaque that was unveiled by Prince Edward, the Earl of Wessex, on June 7, 2005.

The first tower of the new Toronto-Dominion Centre changed the city skyline forever. Note the original concept of the CN Tower to the left of this doctored photo. The idea of a three-legged structure was deemed impractical for a variety of reasons.

Driving Ambition

In a recent edition of *Canadian Driver*, Canada's online automotive magazine, there was a feature listing the various manufacturers who build vehicles in Canada. In addition to General Motors (Oshawa), Ford (Oakville), and Chrysler (Brampton and Windsor), Honda, Suzuki, and Toyota have factories in Alliston, Ingersoll, and Cambridge respectively. Note that while all of these factories are in Ontario, none is located in Toronto.

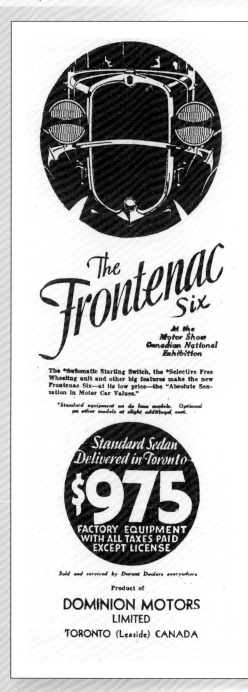

Newspaper ad announcing the 1932 Leaside-built Frontenac "6-85."

Interestingly, over the years our city has been home to a variety of auto plants. Aside from the one-off models that appeared early in the twentieth century, several of the large American manufacturers opened branch plants in Toronto.

There was the Dodge Brothers factory at the southwest corner of Dupont and Dufferin. Not far away, the Russell Motor Car Company built the exceptional Russell automobile in a sprawling factory on Weston Road north of St. Clair. It's been said that the Russell was the first financially successful Canadian-built automobile.

But the Russell operation eventually went out of business, and the Willys-Overland Company of Toledo, Ohio, took over the factory. This company's Knight and Whippet models were extremely popular, but the Great Depression ended all that and the company closed its Toronto operations at the end of 1933.

Even Ford had assembly plants in Toronto. The first opened in 1916 at the northwest corner of Dupont and Christie (that building is still there—its roof was the test track). It was eventually replaced by a newer place out on Danforth near Victoria Park. When Ford moved out of that one, Nash moved in. Nash, now part of American Motors, left Toronto in 1957, the building then becoming part of the Shopper's World complex.

One of the most interesting vehicle manufacturing operations was that of "Billy" Durant, who had founded General Motors only to lose control, regain it, and lose it for a second and final time in 1920. Undaunted, Durant established a new company using his own name and opened a Canadian branch in a former munitions plant in the Toronto suburb of Leaside.

The first Canadian-built Durant rolled off the line in early 1922. The company also sold a less-expensive model called the Star. Interestingly, the local firm managed to do better than the parent, and when Durant south of the border failed, all its assets were acquired by the newly established Dominion Motors Ltd. Joining the Durant lineup in 1931 was a new model called the Frontenac, so named in honour of the governor of New France in the late seventeenth century. Dominion also added REO Speed Wagons and Rugby trucks to its inventory.

Company officials hoped for great things, but it wasn't to be. By the end of 1933, all production at the Leaside plant had ended. Some years later, Canada Wire and Cable occupied the factory, and more recently the multi-faceted complex was demolished. Several big box stores now occupy much of the site, but the Durant Company's office building still stands across the street.

Aerial view showing Durant car factory on the east side of Laird Drive at Wicksteed in suburban Leaside, circa 1931. This property is now covered by several big box stores.

FILEY *Fact*

After months of hype, the Ford Motor Company unveiled its newest model, the Edsel, to the public at the 1957 edition of the Canadian National Exhibition, an event that took place on September 2 in the Automotive Building. That was two days before the rest of the world saw the car for the first time. Before the name Edsel was selected (to honour Edsel, late son of the company founder), the name Utopian Turtletop was suggested.

Not at Your Service

I have a question: Is it possible that because there are so few brands of gasoline out there those who are in business can charge more for their product? Just asking.

You know, it doesn't seem all that long ago that automobile drivers had a wide array of gasoline brands to choose from. Remember these guys—White Rose, Lion, Joy, Premium, Reliance, British-American, Gulf, Texaco, Regent, and Fina? I'm sure there were others. One that I have particular memories of was a neighbourhood gas station on Mount Pleasant Road at Broadway in North Toronto run by Harry Norman and Jan Wietzes that proudly identified itself as part of "Canada's All-Canadian Company." While there were a number of Supertest stations around town (including one at the intersection of Vaughan Road and Bathurst Street), I remember Harry and Jan's place with great fondness, since it was there that I bought my first car, a used 1958 Hillman Minx, an English-built car that wouldn't start if the newspaper even suggested it might rain sometime during the next week.

Supertest was created by John Gordon Thompson, who had been in the service station equipment business in London, Ontario, in the early 1920s, selling machinery for repairing tires and other types of garage equipment as well as the

Undated photo of the Supertest gas station at the intersection of Bathurst Street and Vaughan Road.

Same view today. Note the Wychwood branch of the public library to the extreme right.

state-of-the-art "visible" gasoline pumps such as those seen in the old photo. Realizing he could only sell to his customers every 10 or so years, he decided to get into the gasoline business. In 1923 he bought a rundown station in downtown London and, after fully refurbishing it, reopened it under the Supertest banner. Five year later he moved into the Toronto market. The key to Thompson's ultimate success was using two neatly uniformed attendants to look after each customer when his or her car rolled up to the pumps. One attendant would pump the gas while the other checked the oil, radiator, and tires before cleaning the windshield. Failure to perform any of those tasks meant the customer received the purchase free.

While other gasoline company officials laughed, Supertest stations became busier and busier so that by the mid-1930s the firm was employing more than 500 people, had over 100 trucks on the road serving nearly 5,000 consumer accounts, and was supplying gasoline to 342 Supertest-branded stations throughout Ontario and Quebec.

For reasons I don't fully understand (well, I think I do, but I better not put them in print), Supertest was sold to British Petroleum (remember BP?) in 1971, a company that was in turn acquired by today's Petro-Canada 12 year later. And now there are four.

Public Power

"Power to the People" was the cry heard around the province more than 100 years ago. Citizens were fed up with paying a few businessmen exorbitant prices for electricity, especially when a good portion of that power was being generated using a public commodity—the fast-flowing waters cascading over the Canadian Falls at Niagara.

One person trying to do something about it was Toronto alderman Francis Spence. He attempted to convince the provincial government to give his city the authority to develop a municipally owned utility that would generate electricity at Niagara Falls, then transmit it to Toronto where it would be sold to consumers at cost. Spence was rebuffed on three occasions, but his fourth attempt in 1902 resulted in a breakthrough. Although Toronto still wasn't permitted to establish its own power utility, the province did agree that it would look favourably on such a request if it was put forward by a group of municipalities. The following year saw 16 communities band together, and soon the fight for public ownership of the province's water resources was underway.

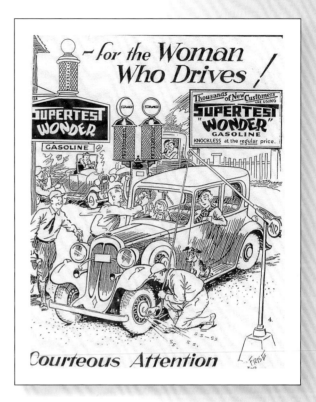

It all came to a head more than a century ago when 1,500 delegates (with Alderman Spence still interested but now in the background) from 70 municipalities across southern Ontario congregated in front of Toronto's Old City Hall and—after a series of high-spirited speeches—marched along Queen Street and up University Avenue to the Legislative Buildings. There they were warmly received by Premier Whitney and Adam Beck, a member of Whitney's Conservative Party and a strong advocate of "cheap power"—the very words emblazoned on the oversize badges worn by the marchers. Less than a month later "An Act for the Transmission of Electric Power to the Municipalities" was introduced by the government. Its subsequent passage resulted in the creation of what became known as Ontario Hydro, with

Adam Beck as its first chairman. Public ownership was set aside in 1998 with the passage of the Energy Competition Act and the subsequent competitive electricity marketing that soon followed.

With the creation of Ontario Hydro in 1906, it wasn't long before this new organization was producing and distributing most of the electricity to consumers and businesses throughout the province. For a time it appeared there would always be a surplus of power. However, one of the most serious tests of Ontario Hydro's ability to keep the lights on and the machinery running occurred following the end of the Second World War. The return of good times soon saw demand for power outstripping generating capacity. In Toronto citizens began to suffer through frequent "brownouts," and restrictions on the use of electricity soon included the prohibition of Christmas lights.

In this 1971 photograph the mammoth R.L. Hearn Generating Station's towering 705-foot chimney is almost complete.

To help alleviate this shortage, several thermal plants were constructed, including a massive coal-fired generating station on Toronto's eastern waterfront. It was named in honour of Richard Lancaster Hearn, who had joined the commission in 1913 following his graduation from the University of Toronto. During his long career, he held numerous positions, starting as a junior draftsman and eventually rising to Ontario Hydro's top job as chairman in which capacity he served in 1955 and 1956. Dr. R.L. Hearn died in 1987 at the age of 97.

The Hearn plant first began generating electricity in late October 1951, with seven additional generating units added over the next decade. In response to concerns over air pollution from the burning of coal, the Hearn facility was converted to natural gas in 1971–72 and a towering 705-foot chimney was erected to better disperse the pollutants. The plant was taken out of service in the summer of 1979, with the last two units shut down four years later.

With a predicted shortage of electricity once again facing the Greater Toronto Area, Ontario is recommending the construction of a 550-megawatt "natural gas–fuelled combined cycle power generation facility" to be known as the Portlands Energy Centre on a site just east of the Hearn. Others are promoting a smaller gas-fired facility to be constructed inside the abandoned Hearn. There may be life in the old place yet.

Today the Hearn Generating Station sits mothballed. The province's new Portlands Energy Centre is proposed for a site just east of the Hearn.

Snapshot of the Past

The other day I was going through a bunch of photographs I took many years ago. Suddenly, I realized that most of them are now of the "historic" variety. That got me to thinking about the time I bought my first half-decent camera. Being a student at Ryerson, I really didn't have a lot of money. Maybe a used camera would be the best choice, perhaps from one of those second-hand places down on Queen Street near Old City Hall. One place I remember visiting was called Henry & Co. It was squeezed between a sporting goods store and a second-hand junk shop on the south side of Queen Street just east of the York Street corner. When I entered, the man behind the counter knew instinctively that I was a neophyte with absolutely no skill in the art of buying used goods. As it turned out, that didn't really matter, because he sold me a camera at a price I could afford, one that served me well until I could purchase something better.

Now, in case you haven't made the connection, the Henry & Co. shop that I visited nearly 50 years ago was the forerunner of today's huge Henry's photographic organization. Interestingly, but for a quirk of fate, what today is known far and wide as Henry's might just as easily have been called Harry's. And here's why ...

Founder Harry
(Henry) Stein
in 1914.

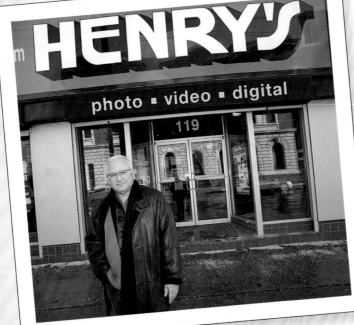

Henry's chairman and
CEO Andrew Stein.
(Courtesy Sam Wong)

Young Harry Stein was employed by the Trans-Siberian Railway where his job was to keep the all-important timekeeping instruments in good running order. In the early 1900s, Harry decided to seek his future in Canada and chose the small city of Toronto as his new home.

By 1909 Harry was able to save enough money to open a small watch repair and jewellery shop in the city's west end—no mean feat for a man who spoke very little English. As the years went by, Harry changed his business address several times, eventually winding up (sorry) in the early 1930s at 63 Queen Street West, a few steps away from the busy Bay Street corner.

It was about this time that Harry, who was never really happy with his given first name, changed it to Henry. From now on the business would be known as Henry & Co. Then, in the early 1940s, Harry moved again, this time to 111 Queen Street West, the small shop where I bought my first camera.

In 1958 Henry's (or is it Harry's?) son, Gerald, and his wife, Adele, took over running the store. It was Gerry, as I came to know him, who introduced the first photographic products (a few rolls of movie film) to the list of items offered for sale at Henry & Co.

Business in 1964 was good, and Henry & Co. was on the move

again, this time to 135 Church Street just north of the Queen Street corner. Jewellery, watches, and musical instruments were dropped from the inventory, and the company began specializing in photographic equipment.

The company continued to expand, and by 1974 it was obvious that a larger store was necessary. The company purchased the former McBride furniture store down the street at 119 Church Street, and it became the new home of what was now known simply as Henry's. In 1983 the founder's grandson, Andrew Stein, who had worked part-time in his parents' store while going to school and university, purchased the company. Andy is now the chairman and CEO of Henry's.

Luxury Up on High

Today it's just another one of Toronto's towering skyscrapers. And, except for the fact that it's empty, it's not unlike many of the city's other tall office buildings. But when it opened more than 50 years ago it was the "cat's meow." In fact, the building was so special it even offered public tours. To get admission tickets, though, you had to obtain them in advance at a gas station. Hmm, now what building could I be talking about?

Sitting prominently on the escarpment that crosses the city in an east-west direction just above Davenport Road is the still-handsome former head office building of Imperial Oil Limited. It rises on the south side of St. Clair between Yonge Street and Avenue Road. Void of tenants since company personnel relocated to other Toronto-area buildings, with some going as far west as Calgary, its future is, you should pardon the expression, "up in the air."

In fact, I was advised by an Imperial Oil official that once the remediation of the surrounding property has been completed, the building and surrounding site will be put up for sale. Will it remain an office building or be converted into an upscale condominium? That's anybody's guess. But buyer beware, because of its architectural significance, the structure is on the city's list of heritage properties.

Designed by the prominent Canadian architectural firm of Mathers and Haldenby, the 21-storey Imperial Oil Building had the distinction of being the highest point

The Imperial Oil Building under construction in 1956.

Now vacant, the Imperial Oil Building still dominates the St. Clair Avenue West streetscape. The future of this handsome building is unknown.

in the entire city when the structure opened over 50 years ago. That's because, even though the building is only 295 feet high, it stands on a remarkable geological feature that delineates the shoreline of the ancient Lake Iroquois of some 12,000 years ago, which can be seen as a steep hill on most of the city's major north-south traffic arteries. As a result, the Imperial Oil head office actually towered over Toronto's tallest building in the 1950s, the 34-storey Bank of Commerce near the King and Yonge corner in the heart of the city.

The actual construction of the oil company's new head office, which would replace its former headquarters in the old Toronto Railway Company Building at the northwest corner of King and Church streets, set a record by being the largest all-welded steel-frame structure in the world. In fact, the building was unique enough to draw engineers, architects, artists, and industrial designers from all over the world, each of whom was eager to have a closer look at Esso's new office tower.

In a newspaper article that described the building, it was reported that the structure was one of the best-equipped office buildings in the world. There were 900 telephones, each of which had the capability of being converted to the space-age "video-phones" once this technology was perfected. Remember, this was 1957. Mail was to be sorted in the basement, then sent throughout the building in baskets placed on conveyor belts that would run vertically up through openings in each floor. Individual baskets of mail would be ejected from the belt automatically onto receiving platforms at the appropriate floor. Upon the mail's arrival, a light on the receptionist's desk would signal a staff member to pick up the letters and packages and distribute them to individuals on that floor.

Another modern feature of the building was the regulation of its interior temperature using heated or chilled water passing through tubes in the ceiling and under the windows in each and every room. Water was also employed in tubes surrounding the hundreds of high-intensity fluorescent lighting fixtures. As the lights heated up, a thermostat in the tube opened, allowing chilled water to cool the air surrounding the fixture.

So proud was the owner of the new building that members of the public were invited to tour the structure after business hours during early July 1957. But so as not to miss a trick, passes to gain admission to the building had to be picked up at ... wait for it ... the local Imperial Esso gas station.

Gas Pains

In what now seems like the very distant-past, I filled up at a local Petro-Canada gas station where the price had dropped to 93 cents a litre. I can well remember, though, that when I was still in high school, I would gas up my first car, a 1958 Hillman Jinx, I mean, Minx, with gas selling at a price using those same two figures, but they were transposed ... not 93 cents but 39 cents ... and that was for a whole gallon of the stuff! Who would have thought that someday 93 cents a litre would be regarded as cheap?

While on the subject of Petro-Canada, that brand didn't exist when I was tooling around town in that old Hillman. But one of the gas companies that I frequented did eventually become part of the huge Petro-Canada family.

On the west side of Mount Pleasant Road, at the southwest corner of Erskine, was a British American (B/A) station operated by a fellow named Powell, a name I had forgotten until Wally Clayson, who ran the Shell station a block farther north and who now has the Master Mechanic garage on Laird Drive in Leaside, reminded me of it.

The British American Oil Company (B/A) was established over 100 years ago by A.L. Ellsworth, a successful Canadian entrepreneur who eventually moved into the large residence on Wilson Avenue at the northeast corner of Yonge Boulevard that is now part of the Canadian Officers Staff College. Originally, his company processed crude oil into a variety of lubricants and greases for the railway industry

Pigott Construction, the builder of the new $8 million Imperial Oil head office on St. Clair Avenue West, placed this ad in Toronto's *Telegram* newspaper a few months before the building opened in July 1957.

Imperial Oil station at Eglinton Avenue and Oriole Parkway in the late 1940s.

and also made a product called kerosene, something that was used primarily as an illuminating fuel.

The cracking process also resulted in another product, one that was virtually useless. With so few vehicles with internal combustion engines around town, this "gasolene"—as it was originally known—was virtually impossible to sell. In fact, the demand was so small that the smelly stuff was simply disposed of in a swampy area adjacent to the company's refinery on the north side of Keating Street (today's Lake Shore Boulevard East) just east of Cherry Street.

Of course, as the internal combustion engine automobile became more popular, the market for gasoline began to increase. What had been a waste by-product was now a new source of income for the company. Initially, B/A sold its product to a variety of outlets, including stables, blacksmith shops, general garages, and even hardware stores. It wasn't until 1925 that B/A opened its first company-owned service station at the southeast corner of Bloor and Delaware streets in west-central Toronto.

Soon there were B/A gasoline stations throughout the nation—each with the familiar B/A "bow tie" logo that was eventually supplanted by a circular red-and-green logo that had the letters *B* and *A* superimposed over reversed oil droplets.

In 1969 B/A was purchased by the giant American oil conglomerate Gulf Oil, and before long the familiar B/A signs were replaced by Gulf signs. Gulf Canada's refining and retailing operations were purchased in 1985 by Petro-Canada, a Crown corporation set up by

Meet Mr. B-A

the Canadian government in 1975 to, as revealed on the company's website, "create a strong Canadian presence in the oil industry and identify new Canadian energy resources."

Petro-Canada went on to absorb two other gasoline companies whose stations were once familiar sights on Toronto-area streets. Fina became part of Petro-Canada in 1981, with BP being absorbed two years later. In 1995 government plans to privatize Petro-Canada were finalized.

Another long-time Canadian gasoline company, British American Oil, ran out of gas in 1969.

5

Toronto and Disaster

Our City in Ruins

On April 23, 1904, the air in downtown Toronto was still thick with smoke as officials began surveying the fire-ravaged buildings on Bay, Wellington, and Front streets. The conflagration that had erupted four days earlier in the old Currie neckwear factory on the north side of Wellington, steps west of Bay, had destroyed more than 100 buildings and in doing so had forced nearly 6,000 people out of work. Many felt that the destruction of so many important businesses would result in Toronto losing its status as the province's principal city. Some even suggested that Hamilton would soon assume that exalted role.

City officials, eager to clear the area and get on with the rebuilding of the city's heart, put out a call asking those with experience in the use of dynamite to help with the demolition of the dozens and dozens of ruined structures. One person who answered the call was 30-year-old John Croft, who had recently immigrated to Canada from England. One of his jobs back home was as a coal miner, where he had watched and occasionally assisted others who used explosives to open new seams.

With a wife and three children to look after, Croft—who could certainly use the extra money being offered to help dynamite the ruins—approached those in charge and after some discussion was assigned the task of demolishing the fire-scarred walls of the W.J. Gage Building at 54–58 Front Street West. Three sticks of dynamite should do it, Croft thought, and he proceeded to place the charges strategically. Unfortunately, one thing Croft lacked was a storage battery, the use of which was the proper and safe way to set off the charges. Instead, he would have to employ long fuses that he would set alight with a match, then run for cover. That procedure worked fine for the first two sticks. The third, however, failed to explode. It must be a dud, he reasoned. After waiting a few minutes to be sure, Croft approached the area where he

One of the Toronto Fire Department's steam fire engines belches smoke as it pumps water to help extinguish the searing flames that destroyed much of downtown Toronto on April 19 and 20, 1904.

had inserted the stick of dynamite. Suddenly, it went off, pummelling poor Croft with large chunks of brick and knocking him unconscious. He was quickly removed to the Emergency Hospital located on the east side of Bay Street just north of the fire zone. Mrs. Croft and the children were sent for but upon arrival at the hospital were advised that John was in serious condition and not expected to survive.

Early the following morning, May 5, 1904, the unfortunate John Croft died from his injuries, the first and only victim of the Great Toronto Fire of 1904. He was buried two days later in Mount Pleasant Cemetery's Plot P—Lot 2242.

Rare Photos of the Great Toronto Fire

Torontonians wandering into the downtown area of their city on April 22, 1904, would have been confronted with scenes of total destruction such as those captured in these rare photographs. The picture below looks south down Bay Street across Wellington Street.

Looking south down Bay Street across Wellington Street. Water is still being poured into the ruined building of the W.R. Brock Company, a prominent city dry goods dealer.

The photo opposite looks west along Wellington Street toward Bay; downed hydro and telegraph wires, which seriously impeded the firemen, criss-cross the intersection. Close inspection of the pavement in the foreground shows how the heat of the inferno caused it to heave. The photo below looks west along Wellington Street toward Bay

Street. Notice the mounted policeman to the right no doubt keeping an eye on curious citizens. In the distance, firefighting equipment can be seen pouring water on the rubble and shells of buildings that once lined Wellington.

Toronto's Worst Disaster

It was on September 16, 1949, that the largest passenger ship plying the waters of the Great Lakes glided through the Western Gap and into Toronto Harbour. The *Noronic* was an infrequent visitor to the provincial capital, with its primary routes being between cities on Lakes Erie, Michigan, and Superior. That was because early in the ship's career, visits to Lake Ontario ports were impossible, since the old Welland Canal (the third canal) wasn't big enough to accommodate large vessels like the *Noronic*. It wasn't until the present, or fourth, canal was completed that the *Noronic* was able to venture farther east. However, with the enlargement of the old locks along the St. Lawrence River still years in the future, Prescott and the Thousand Islands situated at the east end of Lake Ontario would remain the vessel's easternmost limits.

The Great Lakes passenger ship SS *Noronic* was known as the "Queen of the Lakes." Usually seen cruising on the upper lakes, this beautiful vessel made its first visit to Toronto on June 10, 1931. Here the ship is seen traversing the Welland Canal.

Although the *Noronic*'s arrival in Toronto early on the evening of September 16, 1949, drew a curious crowd to the waterfront, the event was nothing like the vessel's first visit to the provincial capital 18 years earlier. On that occasion more than 20,000 spectators rushed to the city's bustling waterfront to inspect a ship that in the 18 years that had passed since its launching on June 3, 1913, at the Port Arthur, Ontario, shipyard of the Western Drydock and Shipbuilding Company had earned the title "Queen of the Lakes." The new vessel's name, *Noronic*, was created using letters in the words *(No)rthern Navigation* and *(R)ichelieu* and *(On)tario*—two companies that eventually became part of Canada Steamship Lines—plus the suffix *ic* as employed on all Northern Navigation vessels. The ship entered service in 1914 as the flagship of the Northern Navigation Company. Nearly 400 feet in length, the

Noronic was licensed to carry 600 first-class and 240 second-class passengers while requiring a crew complement of 200. An important safety feature was that her five decks were made of steel.

Over the next several decades the *Noronic* safely carried thousands of fun-seeking passengers on numerous trips between ports in Canada and the United States. In fact, the popular vessel's visit to Toronto nearly 60 years ago was simply one component of a late-season cruise that was to take passengers from Michigan and Ohio to the Thousand Islands and back. The *Noronic* was to stay in Toronto until Saturday afternoon, then continue its voyage down the lake. Unfortunately, for the 524 passengers and 171 crew members onboard, that trip would end suddenly and with great sadness during the ship's Toronto stay.

All appeared normal as the *Noronic*'s passengers turned in for the night and the ship lay safely berthed at the foot of Yonge Street. Most of the crew also got some shuteye, though a few stood the night watch.

Sometime after 2:00 a.m. smoke was discovered seeping under the door of a linen closet out into one of the companionways. Feeble attempts were made to smother the flames but to no avail and within minutes the entire area was ablaze.

Over the years SS *Noronic* made several visits to the Port of Toronto. During its visit in 1949, it was destroyed by fire at the foot of Yonge Street. This conflagration has the dubious distinction of being the worst disaster in Toronto's history.

Years of paint and varnish applied throughout the ship's interior gave the flames a head start, and it wasn't long before the vessel's fate was sealed. Men and equipment from the Toronto Fire Department rushed to the scene, but all they could do was pour thousands of gallons of water on the inferno while trying desperately to get people off the ship. The drama played out all through the night, and when the flames were finally extinguished, all that was left to do was count and identify the victims. And that wasn't an easy job, since many had been burned beyond recognition. The remains were moved to a temporary morgue in the CNE's Flower Building and pioneering forensic techniques were utilized, but the process took time. Eventually, however, most victims were identified. A few weren't, and those remains were interred in a grave in Mount Pleasant Cemetery.

Weeks passed and the death toll continued to rise. It topped out at 118, a number that made the disaster at the foot of Yonge Street the worst in the city's history. A month later that horrific number was increased by one when one of the injured succumbed to her burns in a Sarnia hospital; she had the dubious distinction of being the only Canadian victim.

Up in Smoke

Over the years many buildings on the grounds of the Canadian National Exhibition have been lost to fire. One structure that remains indelibly etched in my mind is the Transportation Building, later renamed the Business Machines Building, then renamed once again years later when it featured goods and treasured *antiques* from Spain.

It was in this guise that the 1908 structure burned to the ground just days after the 1974 CNE got underway. I remember this event particularly well, since I had started working at the CNE earlier that year. Looking at the smouldering ruins of a once-proud building is a sight I won't soon forget.

By the way, the reason I put the word *antiques* in italics is that while we all thought many of the special items on display in the building were supposedly rare

In 1999 the Ontario Heritage Foundation erected this commemorative plaque just west of the Yonge Street slip, the site of the *Noronic* disaster a half-century earlier.

The Manufacturers' Building (circa 1902), where the latest in consumer goods were on display, was a popular attraction at the annual Canadian National Exhibition.

All that remains of the old Manufacturers' Building after a devastating fire that erupted on January 3, 1962.

artifacts, they were, in fact, only replicas—items of little or no value.

An earlier fire totally destroyed a building that at the time was the largest on the CNE grounds. The Manufacturers' Building had been completed in time for the 1902 edition of the fair, an annual event that back then was still known as the Toronto Industrial Exhibition. Ten years later officials authorized a change in the fair's title to the Canadian National Exhibition to better describe an attraction that, since its inception in 1879, had become truly national in scope. So influential was the annual exhibition that many Canadian manufacturing concerns sought a special building in which they could present their products to potential customers who were eager to have the latest appliances, furniture, and other consumer goods. Two of the major tenants were the T. Eaton Company and the Robert Simpson Company, who at the time were Canada's leading retailers, especially of items that were collectively referred to as "home furnishings." As we all now know, neither of these long-time companies remain in business today, Simpson's having become part of the Hudson's Bay organization in 1978, while Eaton's was swallowed up by Sears Canada on December 30, 1999.

So powerful was the annual fair in the early part of the twentieth century that both Eaton's and Simpson's closed their downtown stores for all or part of Saturday during the run of the CNE. People would be encouraged to visit and purchase items from the large Eaton- and Simpson-sponsored displays at the Ex.

Other CNE buildings that have been destroyed by fire include the Crystal Palace and a couple of the grandstands. While the Music Building (built originally in 1908 as the Railways Building) suffered major fire damage in 1987, it has since been restored.

Watery Grave

On the morning of May 29, 1914, Canadians were just getting the news that the nation had suffered the worst maritime disaster in its short 47-year history. With the sinking of the mighty *Titanic* and the horrific loss of life still fresh in most people's minds, the thought that the Canadian Pacific transatlantic liner *Empress of Ireland* had gone to the bottom was almost too much to comprehend.

Postcard view of Canadian Pacific Railway's ill-fated *Empress of Ireland.*

The *Empress*, which had made its maiden trip in 1906, had become one of the most popular ways of crossing the Atlantic, and so the trip departing the Port of Quebec City on the afternoon of May 28, 1914, wasn't regarded by the 1,477 passengers and crew as anything out of the ordinary—except that among the passengers onboard were approximately 170 Salvation Army adherents, including many of the senior officers, as well as 39 members of the Army's Staff Band, which was based in Toronto. All were on their way to an international conference in London, England.

Just hours after the ship's departure, the belief that this would be another "ordinary" transatlantic voyage was shattered when the liner collided with the heavily laden collier *Storstad* as they attempted to pass each other in a dense fog bank that suddenly enveloped a large area of the St. Lawrence River just off Pointe-au-Père. In retrospect, had the *Storstad*, with its bow impaled deep within the liner's starboard side, not backed off but waited until those onboard could escape into the lifeboats, the loss of life would have been much lower. However, the *Storstad*'s captain acted too quickly, and as his ship broke away, thousands of gallons of cold river water rushed into the gaping wound. Within 14 minutes the *Empress* was gone, along with most of its passengers and crew. In fact, the official death toll exceeded 1,000 by 12 poor souls. Interestingly, of that number, 840 were passengers, a tally that exceeded the passenger death toll in the much more famous *Titanic* disaster, which stunned the world and spawned numerous book, poems, records, and movies.

Of the 840 passengers who died in this Canadian disaster, many were Salvationists and many of those victims resided in Toronto. In their honour the Salvation Army holds a memorial service on each Sunday closest to May 29 at the *Empress* monument located just inside the Yonge Street gate to beautiful Mount Pleasant Cemetery. Members of the public are encouraged to attend.

Swept Away

And now the official weather report for Toronto, Hamilton, western Lake Ontario, Niagara, and Georgian Bay for Thursday, October 14, and Friday, October 15, 1954: Thursday, cloudy with occasional showers and thunderstorms. Friday, cooler with clearing late in the afternoon. Winds light.

That was it. A few more hours of rain—it had been raining in the Metro area for the past four or five days—but it looked as if it would finally clear on Friday afternoon.

Boy, did the guys at the weather department miss on that one. Not only did the rain not come to an end as predicted but a weather phenomenon never seen before in Toronto's long history was about to wreak havoc and misery on an unsuspecting community. And when it was over, 81 of the city's citizens would lie dead.

It was at 11:10 p.m. on October 15, 1954, to be coldly precise, that Hurricane Hazel slammed into southern Ontario with disastrous results. Born off the coast of Venezuela on October 6, the eighth tropical storm of the season (in those days hurricanes were named after women—in fact, Hazel followed Gilda and preceded Ida—unlike the present custom of honouring both sexes) began to wander rather aimlessly before ripping apart the western end of the Caribbean island of Hispaniola, leaving 300 Haitians dead and hundreds more injured. Hazel then veered northward and, after narrowly missing the Bahamas, did the unexpected. Instead of heading out to sea, on the morning of October 15, the storm smashed into the U.S. shoreline near Myrtle Beach. Another change in course and now Hazel set her sights on the western end of Lake Ontario and Metro Toronto.

Throughout the day those same forecasters, who just 24 hours earlier hadn't mentioned the hurricane at all in their reports, suddenly decided we were in for a troubling storm of high winds and more rain.

Some of the many localities north of Toronto that suffered huge property losses included Beeton, Brampton, Holland Landing (when the storm finally blew itself out, more than 7,000 acres of rich farmland were underwater), and the ravine called Hogg's Hollow straddling the West Don River at the Toronto–North York Township boundary. To the west a trailer camp at Lakeview near the mouth of Etobicoke Creek was devastated and seven residents got lost in the swirling waters of the normally placid watercourse.

But as bad as the loss of life and property was in those neighbouring communities, nothing equalled the agony, distress, devastation, and misery that assailed the unaware citizens calmly waiting out the storm's fury in their homes on a quiet little street in suburban Weston.

Constructed on the flood plain adjacent to the west bank of the Humber River just south of the Lawrence Avenue bridge, Raymore Drive was flanked by dozens of small two-storey brick homes owned or rented by hard-working, blue-collar workers. In a few cases, elderly retired couples had chosen Raymore Drive as the place to live out the rest of their lives.

In addition to the nearby Lawrence Avenue bridge over the Humber, Westmount—as Raymore Drive and other nearby streets were collectively and officially known—was also served by a small footbridge over the Humber at the point where the river curved slightly. This bridge made trips to the shops on Weston Road easier. It was also to spell doom for many of the Raymore residents.

The days of rain that had preceded the arrival of Hazel had saturated the ground to such an extent that when the new storm let loose there was nowhere for the rain to go but into the nearby watercourses. For miles around Weston all the streams, creeks, and storm sewers fed the Humber, and so as the storm continued to dump its hundreds of millions of gallons of water, the usually tame river was transformed into a raging, unforgiving torrent, with walls of water gouging out new channels regardless of obstructions such

This map, which appeared in the *Evening Telegram*, shows the location of the 17 Raymore Drive houses that were ripped from their foundations by the raging Humber River on October 15, 1954. The dotted lines at the bottom of the view delineate the location of the footbridge that was to cause the tragedy on Raymore Drive. Today this area is Raymore Park.

as trees, outbuildings, concrete abutments, and even a few automobiles that had been swept into the fast-flowing torrent while attempting to cross the river farther upstream.

Some of this flotsam and jetsam careened into the west abutment of the Westmount footbridge, causing the span to fall into the river—now 16 to 20 feet above its normal level. In doing so, the span, still attached at the east end, caused the river to be deflected from its channel and onto Raymore Drive.

Telephone poles, trees, cars, street signs, and whole houses—many with their terrified occupants huddled inside—were suddenly ripped up and sent swirling down the raging river. In all, 17 homes and 1,200 feet of street were obliterated. Worse still, 36 citizens of Raymore Drive died in the split-second tragedy. Of that number, nine were in one house.

6

Toronto Landmarks

FORESTERS TEMPLE, TORONTO.

Toronto's Tower of Power

Anyone 30 years of age or younger will have never known Toronto without the CN Tower gracing the city's skyline. For those of us well over 30, it's difficult to believe the thing's been around for more than three long decades.

While the tower was opened to the public on June 26, 1976, the concept of erecting a super-sized communications tower goes back to Canada's centennial year. In the fall of 1967, Canadian Pacific Railway and Canadian National Railway proposed that as part of their $1 billion redevelopment of the railway lands between Yonge and Bathurst streets south of Front, a 1,500-foot tower be erected specifically to address the Canadian Broadcasting Corporation's requirements for an antenna that would permit better dispersal of its TV signal and eliminate "ghosting" caused by the numerous high-rise buildings erected since the television network's old tower was constructed adjacent to the CBC's studios on Jarvis Street.

And to sweeten the deal it was also proposed that a new broadcasting centre be built as part of the overall project. It could be argued that the whole package was a blatant attempt to lure the CBC away from North York where a site at the northeast corner of the Eglinton–Don Mills Road intersection had been under consideration. Unlike the "one" city we have today, back then the various communities that made up Metro Toronto vied with one another for development.

While the seeds of a mammoth communications tower had been planted, the start of construction was still years in the future, and not everyone wanted the thing built at all. In fact, at its meeting on May 23, 1973, Toronto City Council voted 11–8 against issuing a building permit for the $21 million tower. However, it was determined that because the project was being undertaken by a Crown corporation no permit was actually required. It was a moot point at best, since the first shovels had gone into the ground three and a half months earlier.

In another interesting twist, the billion-dollar Metro Centre project, of which the tower was a key component, would be cancelled even as the yet unnamed tower began to take shape. This drastic step was taken when it became known that the consortium wanted to demolish Union Station and replace it with a modern trans-portation terminal. The citizens of Toronto would have nothing to do with that idea (shades of the "Save Old City Hall" movement). Such interference was the last straw for Bud Andrews, who was spearheading the now $1.5 billion project, and it was decided that the whole thing would be called off.

However, with work on the new communications structure well underway, it was agreed that the tower, at least, would be completed. And with CNR still in the picture, the structure now had a name—the CN Tower.

Oh, one more interesting twist; though it opened more than 30 years ago as the CN Tower, with CN standing for Canadian National (Railway), it no longer operates under that title. Nope, it's now the CN Tower. What? When the railway decided in the mid-1990s to concentrate on the freight business and divest itself of other interests, the Canada Lands Corporation, a Crown corporation that looks after federal real estate development, moved in and changed the name of the landmark to ... wait for it ... Canada's National Tower. So the CN Tower is now the CN Tower.

Pray in Beauty

Toronto has a large inventory of historic places of worship. Some, like Little Trinity (King Street East), the Cathedral Church of St. James (Church Street), Metropolitan (Queen Street East), St. Paul's (Queen Street East), St. Michael's Cathedral (Bond Street), Beth Tzedek (Bathurst Street), and many, many others are well known. However, others that have also been around for decades get little attention.

Take for example St. Luke's at the southeast corner of Carlton and Sherbourne streets just across from Allan Gardens. Its present name is a relatively new one, having been adopted in 1959 when the congregation of what had originally been built in 1887 and known for decades as Sherbourne Street Methodist joined with the displaced congregation of Carlton Street Methodist (United) that was located on the south side of Carlton Street just east of Yonge. This latter church was demolished sometime around 1925. Many of the city's most prominent citizens attended old Sherbourne Street Methodist back when that area of the city was the Forest Hill or Post Road of its day.

Of particular interest in the old postcard view is the horse-drawn sleigh that sits on Sherbourne Street just south of the Carlton corner. This vehicle was one of 100 sleighs operated by the privately owned Toronto Street Railway Company (TSR). The TSR provided horse-drawn streetcar service from 1861 until its successor company the Toronto Railway Company (TRC) took over—after a short but unsuccessful attempt by the city to run the system—in the fall of 1891.

This postcard view, circa 1890, looks east on Carlton Street toward Sherbourne Street after a snow-storm. To the right is the 1887 Sherbourne Street Methodist Church (now St. Luke's United Church). Parliament Street is in the distance.

One of the requirements in the city's agreement with the TSR was that should enough snow fall to impede the ability of its horse-drawn wheeled vehicles to get the job done, horse-drawn sleighs stored in the Front and Frederick streets car house had to be substituted.

It's obvious from the old postcard that the recent storm had dumped enough snow to necessitate the sleighs being called out. However, even more interesting is the fact that there's no horse in front of this particular sleigh. That was because of another rule set out by the streetcar company. While there was virtually no limit on the number of hours the operating staff could be asked to work, there was a limit to the length of time the horses pulling the equipment strained at the reins. Why? Simple. It was easier and cheaper to replace a human who had succumbed to the freezing temperatures (operators stood out in the cold, there being no enclosed vestibule) than it was to replace a departed horse. That replacement could cost the company up to $75. Men, on the other hand, were paid something like 15 cents an hour.

In this view it's likely that the horse that was pulling this sleigh had finished its two hours of work and was on its way back to the barn while a fresh replacement was being trotted up Sherbourne to carry out its two-hour stint.

The same view today.

By the way, we also know that this view wasn't taken on a Sunday. Torontonians couldn't go to Sunday church services on a streetcar until 1897. That was the year the law was changed to permit Sunday streetcar operations.

Postal Past

One of our city's true landmarks has been in the media recently, and for reasons that have little to do with the building's history. Today 10 Toronto Street is home to the Argus Corporation, an investment trust that was incorporated in 1945. In recent years its tenant was the famous, to some infamous, Conrad Black.

Built in 1853, 10 Toronto Street served as Toronto's post office in an era when the city had only two postmen—one for the east side of town, the other for the west. Officially identified as the Seventh Toronto Post Office, it replaced the Sixth down on Wellington Street and was, historically, the lineal successor to Toronto's very first post office located on the north side of Duke Street just east of George. This old building was long forgotten until rescued and resurrected in 1984 by Judy and Sheldon Godfrey. Its modern-day address is 260 Adelaide Street East, and it now operates as ... wait for it ... a vintage post office.

Number 10 Adelaide Street remained the city's main post office until the growing city got a larger facility at the top of Toronto Street in 1872. Sadly, that building was demolished in the late 1950s.

The stately Seventh Toronto Post Office, 10 Toronto Street, circa 1870.

With postal officials gone from 10 Toronto Street for the first time since the building opened in 1853, it wasn't long before another federal government department moved in. This time it was the Ministry of Inland Revenue, which stayed until 1937. Soon thereafter a branch of the Bank of Canada moved in.

For nearly a century, the future of 10 Toronto Street seemed secure—that is, until the bank decided to relocate to its new building on the west side of University Avenue south of Queen in the mid-1950s. Now, with the city undergoing rapid changes, developers began eyeing 10 Toronto Street, not for its historical significance but rather for the site's redevelopment potential. Suddenly, the future of 10 Toronto Street appeared uncertain. Then, in early December 1958, Toronto's *Telegram* newspaper reported that the Argus Corporation was about to give Torontonians what the paper called "a marvellous Christmas present."

Seeking to relocate its corporate headquarters from 15 King Street West, four of the Argus Corporation's directors, E.P. Taylor, Wallace McCutcheon, John "Bud" McDougald, and Eric Phillips, revealed that they had decided to buy 10 Toronto Street. A price wasn't given, but those in the know suggested it would be at least $500,000 "if not more"! Argus planned to restore and renovate the landmark to ensure that, as the *Telegram* stated, "the city would not lose a beautiful and tangible link with the traditions of the past."

Now, after the passage of more than a half-century and the loss of dozens of other stately structures, the actions of these civic-minded businessmen can be appreciated even more.

Prime Real Estate

One of Toronto's few remaining landmark structures, the stately Campbell House at the northwest corner of University Avenue and Queen Street West, was saved from demolition by The Advocates' Society, an organization dedicated to the needs of those who practise advocacy before the courts. In order to accomplish this miracle, it was necessary to move the former residence of Chief Justice William Campbell, which was built in 1822 a full 12 years before Toronto was incorporated as a city, from its original site on Adelaide Street East to a new location. After much discussion, it was decided that a site a mile west of the original location on the lawn south of the Canada Life Building and across from Osgoode Hall, the home of the Law Society of Upper Canada, would afford an appropriate new home. This complicated and Herculean project was accomplished during the Easter long weekend in 1972. Campbell House was officially opened by the Queen Mother a little more than two years later.

But there was no such salvation for another city landmark, one that was—to use a modern-day real estate term—a true townhouse in every sense of that word.

Known far and wide as Cawthra House, the handsome building was erected in 1851 at the northeast corner of King and Bay streets by William Cawthra. It's said that the new owner chose this site for safety—the remoteness of his previous residence in the suburban wilderness near Jarvis and Bloor streets made it easy pickings for vandals.

William was the son of Joseph Cawthra, one of Toronto's earliest and most successful merchants. In fact, Cawthra, who emigrated from Yorkshire, England, in 1803, had received a large land grant many miles to the west of the little Town of York. The location of that property is remembered today in the name of the nearby modern thoroughfare, Cawthra Road, in the City of Mississauga.

It wasn't long after settling on the banks of the Credit River that business interests prompted Joseph to move to York (as Toronto was still called). Over time he acquired substantial town lots, some of which were inherited by his son, William, upon Joseph's death. One of these parcels was at the northeast corner of King and Bay in an area of the young city that was still on the western outskirts of the business section. It was there that William built his new city home. Research indicates the home was designed by Joseph Sheard, an architect of some repute who went on to serve as mayor of Toronto in 1871–72, and was built of Canadian white stone, hand-cut and dressed by master masons. Its interior was trimmed and finished in hand-polished walnut and oak. As one newspaper recorded, "its complete ensemble was the super-product of master builders who were all Canadians."

At the time of William Cawthra's passing in 1880 the old house had become surrounded by a variety of modern (for the day) office buildings. For a time it served as a branch of the Sterling then Molson Bank, but when the mighty Bank of Nova Scotia announced it was going to erect a new head office on the corner, the stately building's days were definitely numbered. There was an attempt to raise funds to relocate all or part of the house and some of its interior fittings, but except for a few bits and pieces that were salvaged, nothing happened and the place was flattened.

In May 1948 hoardings surround the former Cawthra mansion at the northeast corner of King and Bay streets as the date of demolition approaches.

The new building that eventually rose on the site of the old house had a less-than-smooth beginning. It was designed by John Lyle in the late 1920s, but the Great Depression delayed the start of construction, which was further held up by the outbreak of war and the inevitable shortage of materials. Mathers and Haldenby reworked Lyle's plans, and construction finally began in 1946. The dignified Bank of Nova Scotia, to many an architectural equal to the towering Scotia Plaza next door, opened at last in 1951.

Save the Roundhouse

As many *Toronto Sun* readers may be aware, it appears that some sort of arrangement has been struck that will see a major furniture store move into the historic CPR Roundhouse located on Toronto's waterfront near Rogers Centre and the CN Tower. Ever hear of anything so short-sighted? Any wonder our heritage keeps slipping away?

The Royal York Hotel dominates this 1930 skyline view. The newly opened million-dollar CPR Roundhouse can be seen in the foreground.

On October 15, 1929, Canadian Pacific Railway, in need of modern facilities in which to service the increasing number of steam locomotives serving the busy routes into and out of the burgeoning City of Toronto, opened its colossal roundhouse complex near the intersection of Fleet (now Lake Shore Boulevard) and John streets and adjacent to the newly constructed cross-waterfront railway viaduct.

The complex included, in addition to the 32-bay roundhouse, a coaling tower, a water tank, and a huge turntable. That turntable was used to reposition the locomotives after servicing so they would be ready to haul trains eastward. The turntable eliminated the need for a lengthy and costly "turn around" track that otherwise would have been needed to get the locomotives ready for the return trip to Montreal.

These steam-powered trains transported hundreds of thousands of passengers between Montreal and Toronto, Canada's two largest cities. In the days before airliners became the way to travel, trains, pulled by mammoth steam locomotives, were regarded as "King." And if the railway was "King," then the new CPR Roundhouse would be where the King's locomotives would be cleaned, fed, and readied for their daily rounds.

Constructed in only four months, the million-dollar facility was the most modern of its kind on the entire continent. Over the next 30 or so years the CPR Roundhouse, along with a similar Canadian National Railway facility nearby, was kept busy servicing numerous steam engines.

Then, with the advent of more efficient diesel locomotives and the move by Canadian Pacific away from the passenger business, roundhouses became redundant and eventually CN's structure was demolished to make way for the new SkyDome (now Rogers Centre). That left the CPR Roundhouse as a unique artifact in the entire Toronto area, a reminder of a time when steam engines were the workhorses of a proud and fast-growing nation.

In 1984 a report was presented to the city that recommended the CPR Roundhouse be retained and developed into something more than a static museum. In fact, the term *railway interpretive centre* was used to denote an attraction that would complement the other numerous other attractions that were sure to come along as the waterfront evolved from a place of commerce and industry into a destination for both tourists and citizens alike. That same year the city designated the Roundhouse under the Ontario Heritage Act. This action recognized the importance of this structure in the evolution of Toronto. In addition, the complex of buildings was also recognized as a National Historic Site, something important to all of Canada.

As recently as 2006, a report from city staff that amended certain lease arrangements with the Steam Whistle brewery that had become a tenant of a portion of the Roundhouse, confirmed earlier recommendations that the structure, in the report's own words, "be developed as an active museum occupying a significant portion of the roundhouse building. The major component of the museum will be the regular movement of locomotives and rolling stock into and out of the building by means of a fully operational turntable."

Somehow, to the contrary, a deal appears to have been struck that will result in historic locomotives and rail cars being replaced by modern ottomans and recliners. And if that happens, one of the lines in Glenn Miller's 1941 hit song "Chattanooga Choo Choo" might become "nothing could be finer than to be in a recliner."

Seriously, if the city has any interest in Toronto's heritage, it will bounce that furniture showroom idea and start working to fulfill a plan that would turn the CPR Roundhouse into an exciting waterfront attraction.

Hey, I just thought of something. Toronto celebrates its 175th anniversary in 2009. Maybe that dream of a Canadian railway interpretive centre located in the historic CPR Roundhouse can be a legacy of that special year.

The Flatiron Building

A familiar sight when driving or walking through the Front, Wellington, and Church street intersection is to see a group of visitors to our city photographing the "ancient" Gooderham Building (because of its shape some call it the "Flatiron" or "Chocolate Cake" Building) framed by several of the city's modern skyscrapers in the background.

The building's unique shape is a result of the unusual street pattern in that part of the old Town of York. Originally, the western boundary of Old York was George Street, so named to honour the eldest son of King George III, the reigning British monarch. It was an important political ploy for the city's founder, John Graves Simcoe, to recognize royalty back in England. After all, they had great influence on what went on in the New World.

When the town went through its first expansion phase in 1818, the western boundary was moved to Peter Street (Peter Russell, Simcoe's successor). Two of the original trio of east-west streets (Duke, now Adelaide and King) were extended in a straight line. However, the third, Front Street (known for a time as Palace, for the Palace of Government or Parliament Buildings south of the Front and Berkeley intersection), deviated at Church Street (after the pioneer St. James' Church, now the Cathedral Church of St. James) and followed the shoreline of the old Toronto Bay. Its westerly extension was taken up by today's Wellington (named in honour of Arthur Wellesley, the Duke of Wellington).

This resulted in a "gore," which is explained in surveying terminology as "a thin triangular piece of land, the boundaries of which are defined by surveys of adjacent properties." The first substantial structure on the gore was a building known colloquially as the "coffin block" because of its shape and the fact that it was constructed of wood. It is remembered by historians as being the western terminal of the busy Kingston-York stagecoach line.

Purchased by George Gooderham, owner of the highly successful Gooderham and Worts distillery empire east of the foot of Parliament Street (now part of the Distillery District), the old building was soon demolished, and in 1891–92 the present structure was erected.

In the older photograph, we can see the ornate head office of the Bank of Toronto, a financial institution of which Gooderham was a founder (it became part of the Toronto-Dominion Bank in 1955). Located directly north of the Gooderham Building on the northwest corner of Church and Wellington, it was rumoured that a

Looking west on Front Street from Church Street, circa 1880.

Today the Flatiron Building has a backdrop of soaring skyscrapers.

tunnel was constructed between the buildings so Mr. Gooderham, and his money, could get to and from his office and the bank without getting wet.

In the present-day photo, the beautiful old bank building is now the site of a pizza place. At least there's still "dough" on that corner.

T.O. Streets Full of Art

Scattered throughout Toronto are nearly 200 city-owned pieces of outdoor public artwork and historical monuments. They can be found in city parks, adjacent to municipal buildings, and on city streets. They are diverse in their construction and range from bronze and masonry sculptures to works created out of aluminum, polyester resin, stainless steel, and concrete. The oldest item in the collection is the Canadian Volunteers Memorial located on the west side of Queen's Park Circle West, directly opposite the Ontario Legislative Buildings. Also known as the Ridgeway Monument, the work by American artist Robert Reid was unveiled on July 1, 1870, by Sir John Young who, as Lord Lisgar, was serving as the nation's second governor general. Young is also the fellow for whom Lisgar Street in west-central Toronto is named. Fortunately, city officials chose the governor general's title, or we would be faced with two thoroughfares with different spellings but similar pronunciations.

The Canadian Volunteers Memorial, situated on the west side of Queen's Park Circle West, is the oldest in the city. Erected in 1870 to commemorate those who died in the 1866 Fenian Raids, it was also one of Emanuel Hahn's first public creations.

The monument honours those young Canadians who were either wounded or killed during the invasion of Canada by members of the Fenian Brotherhood in 1866. This organization attempted to pressure Great Britain into withdrawing from Ireland by attacking a variety of targets in its colonies in British North America. One of the fiercest incursions took place in early June of that year when a force of nearly 1,500 men, many of them U.S. Civil War veterans, crossed the Niagara River near Fort Erie. Several skirmishes ensued, and by the time the invaders had retreated to the American side of the river, seven members of the Queen's Own Rifles had been killed, with two more eventually succumbing to their wounds. Six more would die as a result of disease contracted during the three-day battle.

In honour of the dead and wounded, a number of influential citizens decided to erect a memorial on the grounds of the University of Toronto. Three of the dead were attending the university when the shocking news of the invasion reached the city. In fact, the name Canadian Volunteers' Memorial was chosen to highlight the fact that many of the dead and wounded were actually citizen soldiers.

Just down the street, in the centre median of University Avenue south of Richmond Street, is another city treasure. This one is passed by thousands of drivers and pedestrians every day, few of whom pay any attention to it. Created by Toronto artist Emanuel Hahn, the Sir Adam Beck Memorial was unveiled on August 15, 1935. The subject of the monument was an early and eager advocate of the public ownership of province-wide electricity-generating and distribution systems.

This enthusiasm eventually led to the creation, in 1906, of the Hydro Electric Power Commission of Ontario, later renamed Ontario Hydro. In 1999 Ontario Hydro was restructured, thereby creating today's Hydro One and Ontario Power Generation. Beck was knighted by King George V in 1914 for his promotion of all aspects of the use of electricity, including high-speed electric "radial" railways such as the one that ran from Toronto to Lake Simcoe in the early 1900s.

Another of Hahn's works is the somewhat peripatetic statue that celebrates Ned Hanlan, the world champion oarsman. When first unveiled in 1926, it stood at the west end of the Canadian National Exhibition grounds. It was then moved to the eastern end, adjacent to what was then the city's popular Marine Museum. In 2004 the statue was moved again, this time to a place of prominence across the bay near the Hanlan's Point ferry docks. While many believe this part of the Toronto Islands was named for Ned, it was, in fact, named for his father, John, who was an early settler of the area that was, up until 1858, the western end of a peninsula.

Hahn's statue of Beck was unveiled at its location in the median of University Avenue just south of Richmond Street on August 15, 1935.

A House Like No Other

Anyone looking at the image that accompanies this column can be forgiven for wondering what a photo of a beautifully landscaped château somewhere in France is doing in an article that usually features items of local history. The fact is that while the building shown has a distinctive European look it is (or should I say was) located in the Rosedale part of Toronto. Known as Government House, it was the second building to serve as the official residence of the lieutenant governor of the Province of Ontario.

The first structure with that lofty title was erected at the southwest corner of King and Simcoe streets (where Roy Thomson Hall stands today) shortly after Ontario came into being following the creation of the Dominion of Canada on July 1, 1867. When first opened, the neighbourhood to the north, south, and west of Government House was residential in nature and was where some of the finest homes in the city could be found on such nearby streets as Mercer, Widmer, Peter, and Wellington. Just across Simcoe Street to the east was the recently constructed Presbyterian Church of St. Andrew, and across King Street to the north was Cawthra Mulock's opulent new Royal Alexandra Theatre.

The last resident of Government House was Dr. Herbert Bruce, who was appointed Ontario's lieutenant governor in 1932. (Photo courtesy Dr. Charles Godfrey)

However, as the years passed, the area became more and more industrialized. When Canadian Pacific Railway announced in early 1911 that it had plans to build a number of railway sheds and numerous sidings just south of the old Government House, officials decided it was time to look for a new site. The first location investigated was on the north side of Bloor Street just east of Yonge. Government officials decided the property offered for sale was too small, and they began looking farther north.

On April 26, 1911, Ontario Premier James Whitney announced that his government had purchased 14 acres of land known as Chorley Park in north Rosedale from the estate of John Hallam for $125,000. Hallam, who as a civic politician championed the public library system we enjoy today, was born in Chorley, Lancashire, England, and had named his suburban land holding after his hometown.

With the site chosen, a location many said was far too remote and far too close to the Don Valley brick-work's belching smokestacks, Francis Heakes, the province's chief archi-tect, was assigned the task of design-ing the new Government House.

Interestingly, even as the initial work was proceeding on the proj-ect, businessman William Gage (Gage Publishing, Gage Institute) offered to sell the province, for the same amount it had spent on Chorley Park, a large parcel of land at the northwest corner of Bathurst and Davenport which, as Gage proposed, would be a perfect spot for the new Govern-ment House. He also suggested that there would be enough room on the property for a public park and a botanical garden. And while the Chorley Park opponents pushed for the government to accept this generous offer, it had arrived too late and the Rosedale project continued.

Government House in Rosedale's Chorley Park was the frequent subject of postcards like this one that promoted "places to see while in Toronto."

Construction went on for more than two years, and by the time Sir John Gibson, Ontario's tenth lieutenant governor, moved in, the cost of the new residence had skyrocketed from an initial $20,000 to nearly $1 million, with the final price (as shown in the Public Works Annual Report for 1917) exactly $1,173,888.

Criticism of the "mansion" had only just begun, and the arrival of the Great Depression only made things worse. Now with hundreds of ordinary citizens going hungry, many began calling for the closure of Government House as a way to save money. The future of the residence became even more clouded when the province's new premier, Mitchell Hepburn, began to feud with Prime Minister William Lyon Mackenzie King. Caught in the middle of some nasty politics was Dr. Herbert Bruce, who had been appointed lieutenant governor in 1932. And while King wanted Government House to remain open, Hepburn eventually won the battle and ordered the place closed at the end of Bruce's term in office, more than 70 years ago.

Over the next few decades the former Government House was used for a variety of purposes, but eventually it fell into such disrepair that its demolition became necessary in 1961. Today Chorley Park is just that—a park.

Since its closure in 1937, the Office of the Lieutenant Governor has occupied several rooms in the Parliament Buildings.

A Pleasant Walk in the Past

While Toronto's beautiful Mount Pleasant Cemetery is the final resting place for more than 200,000 people, many people regard the finely manicured and neatly groomed property on the east side of Yonge Street north of St. Clair Avenue as a history book with the headstones that book's pages.

Mount Pleasant was the third non-sectarian cemetery to be opened by an organization that had originally been created in 1826 to look after those locals and visitors to the town who passed away while here and were not members of either the Roman Catholic Church or Church of England. These two religions provided burial space for their adherents. Virtually all others were out of luck.

The organization's first burial ground opened in 1826 on a six-acre plot of land at the northwest corner of the future Yonge and Bloor Street intersection. Eventually, the burials in what was called Potter's Field began to cause problems for the adjacent Village of Yorkville. The cemetery was stifling the community's growth and the villagers started petitioning provincial officials to have the burial ground closed and the remains removed.

The authorities agreed, and to comply with the government's order that the old cemetery be closed and the remains re-interred elsewhere, what was now called Toronto Trust Cemeteries purchased an existing 15-acre cemetery on the west bank of the Don River at the end of Winchester Street. Trust officials offered the relatives of those buried in the old Potter's Field plots in the newly acquired Necropolis. Many took advantage of the offer, and before long the Yonge and Bloor property was closed.

As the population of the city continued to grow, so, too, did the number of "dear departed." As a result, it wasn't long before the capacity of the Necropolis, too, was being taxed. Anticipating future needs, the Trust sought out additional land on which to develop another burial ground.

In 1873 a 200-acre farm on the east side of Yonge Street several hundred yards north of the little community of Deer Park in the Third Concession from the Bay,

Township of York, was purchased for $20,000. It was soon agreed that this, the third of the Trust's non-sectarian cemeteries, would be called Mount Pleasant.

The concept for the Trust's new cemetery was based on the emerging "landscape style" pioneered by Boston's innovative Mount Auburn Cemetery. Soon what were once farm fields were being transformed into park-like settings complete with trees, shrubs, pathways, and even a small lake. The new Mount Pleasant Cemetery became such a departure from the ordinary type of churchyards and burial grounds that it soon became a featured item in the city's daily newspapers. In fact, the cemetery was seen as an attraction of such uniqueness that the local guidebooks recommended a visit north of the city to witness its wonders. One publication was very specific, commenting that "No visit to Toronto will be complete without a visit to Mount Pleasant Cemetery. The cars of the Metropolitan Street Railway run right to the main entrance."

Mount Pleasant Road in the early days of the cemetery.

On the afternoon of November 4, 1876, a little more than two years after the Trustees purchased what was just one of the many rambling farms that surrounded the young city of Toronto, the public arrived in huge numbers to attend the official opening of Toronto's Mount Pleasant Cemetery.

And the Winner Was ...

When it was decided in 1880 that Ontario needed a new building to replace the old Parliament Building, an ancient structure on Front Street West (that stood where the CBC Building is today), it was agreed that the site of the new building would be at the head of Queen Street Avenue (a thoroughfare we now call University). This choice would mean that the old Provincial Lunatic Asylum that had started out as King's College, the forerunner of the present University of Toronto, would have to be demolished. It was also decided that the design of such an important building would be selected through an international competition.

In 1880 an international competition was held to come up with a design for Ontario's new Legislative Buildings. This work, from Toronto architects Darling and Curry, won that competition, but was never built.

The new Legislative Buildings of Ontario as completed in 1893.

A total of 16 architectural firms entered the contest, with the first-, second-, and third-place winners, all of which were local firms, being awarded $2,000, $1,000, and $500 respectively. But a number of things associated with the winning design of Darling and Curry were subsequently found to be "unsuitable" and a second competition between the first- and second-place winners was held in 1882. That, too, was inconclusive. The government, deciding that because neither design was "suitable" (the terms *unsuitable* and *suitable* were never fully defined), awarded Richard Waite, an English architect living in Buffalo, a contract to build the project at a cost "not to exceed $750,000." Waite was also a member of the selection committee, and it was rumoured that he had close ties with several high-ranking bureaucrats and politicians. The newspapers attempted to make the government's strange handling of the project a "hot news story," but that, too, failed. Waite's contract was dated January 8, 1886.

The new Parliament Buildings of Ontario opened with great pomp and ceremony on April 4, 1893. Oh, and the final cost—nearly twice the budgeted figure of $750,000.

The first premier to work in the new building was Sir Oliver Mowat. He served as premier for an incredible 24 years (1872–1896). Mowat was subsequently appointed Ontario's ninth lieutenant governor (1897–1903).

Battle for Sunnybrook

Toronto is fortunate to have a fine selection of hospitals staffed by highly trained doctors and nurses as well as hundreds of caring volunteers. One of the busiest of these hospitals is what we now know as Sunnybrook and Women's College Health Sciences Centre on Bayview Avenue just south of Lawrence.

It was on June 12, 1948, that its immediate predecessor, the much-beleaguered Sunnybrook Military Hospital, was officially opened. I say beleaguered because initially no one in high places had any intention of building the place. That's because it was generally felt by those in charge of looking after the medical and psychological needs of returning Second World War veterans that the existing hospitals scattered across the nation, including the primary military hospital of the day located on Christie Street just north of Dupont (now the site of Christie Gardens retirement home), were more than up to the task.

Thankfully, there were many prominent citizens who had a different opinion. In fact, they were virtually unanimous in condemning "Christie Street" as totally inappropriate as a veterans' hospital for a variety of reasons. The most important reason was that the place was actually built in the early teens as an assembly factory for the National Cash Register Company and now it was simply being requisitioned by the federal government of the day as a kind of "refuge" for vets returning from the Great War. Actually, the building's location was perfect for use as a factory. The tracks over which belching, noisy steam locomotives operated to bring the hundreds of necessary parts to build cash registers were right next door. But when the factory was converted to hospital use, those same belching, noisy trains had no place being that close to where rest and quiet were the required medicines. In addition, as a factory, the layout of the floors, staircases, et cetera, would have been perfect. As a hospital, it was next to impossible to provide the necessary

Ontario's Legislative Buildings today.

operating and recovery rooms while maintaining the sterile conditions required for proper recuperation.

However, the government insisted Christie Street would suffice. Until a number of prominent Torontonians forced the issue, that is. And to show its concern that its returning boys get the best possible treatment, the City of Toronto even offered to provide the land on which a new specially designed veterans' hospital could be built. This is where the late Joseph Kilgour's Sunnybrook Farm enters the picture. This beautiful piece of property, 178 acres in size and valued at $350,000, had been given to the city in 1926 as a public park by Joseph's widow, Alice, on the condition that it be retained as a park for the enjoyment of visitors and never be developed commercially.

City officials believed that the park would be a perfect location for the new hospital. However, since Alice had passed away, permission had to be sought from the Kilgour estate to allow a hospital to be built on a portion of the property. The necessary permission was granted, and on November 11, 1943, the first sod for the new structure was turned.

Exactly two years later, on November 11, 1945, Corporal Fred Topham, VC (whose medal was the topic of a country-wide fundraising campaign to keep it in Canada), laid the cornerstone of the new Active Treatment

Sunnybrook Military Hospital soon after it opened on June 12, 1948.

Building. Nevertheless, shortages of both materials and labour meant that the hospital wasn't ready for its first patients until the fall of 1946, long after the war had ended. Another 20 months would pass before the official opening in the presence of Prime Minister Mackenzie King took place.

Child Full of Grace

In 1889, just seven years after the Salvation Army made its first appearance on the not-too-friendly streets of Toronto, its members opened a "rescue home" in the former residence of prominent city businessman Edward Leadley. Leadley was president of Standard Woollen Mills and built his magnificent house, which still stands at 25 Augusta Street (its original address was 17 Esther Street), in 1876. After serving the community for 16 years, the home was finally recognized formally by the provincial government on October 15, 1905, as the Salvation Army Maternity Hospital. Four years later the hospital moved again, this time to a location not far from the Yonge and Bloor intersection where it re-established itself in another former residence, this time that of the Bloor family. This family's patriarch was none other than Joseph Bloor (spelled Bloore if the inscription on his headstone in the Necropolis is to be believed), who began his working career tending bar in the Farmers' Arms near the old St. Lawrence Market, moved to the countryside north of the city where he opened a brewery, then went on to develop much of the early Village of Yorkville with William Botsford Jarvis, the "father" of Rosedale.

An extension was added in 1925 to what Torontonians now knew as the Toronto Women's Hospital. A dozen years later that name was changed to the now-familiar Grace Hospital. Here, thousands of babies first saw the light of day, a proud group to be sure and one that includes myself. Oh, how well I remember coming into the world that Saturday, October 11, 1941, with my mother and father gazing at their first born while I stared out the windows at the Bloor streetcars. Maybe that's when it all started ...

A new Grace Hospital was constructed in 1959 around the corner on Church Street, and the old Bloor (or is it Bloore?) house was demolished. A decade passed, and what had been a maternity hospital for more than 60 years was re-designated a general hospital. That designation changed once again in 1979 when the Grace became a chronic care and palliative care facility. In 1998 the powers that be tried to close the hospital only to have the Ontario Ministry of Heath reverse that decision three years later.

From its start as a maternity hospital more than a century ago to the compassionate palliative and chronic care the hospital provides today, Toronto Grace Hospital has served life's full spectrum from beginning to end.

Defending Fort York

I'm often asked my opinion as to what is the most important historic site in Toronto. Without hesitation I reply Fort York. But there was a time when the powers that be wanted the old fort moved. Why? Because it was in the way of the new Gardiner Expressway.

But first things first: Why do I think the fort is such an important icon in the history of Toronto? And why is it there in the first place? To answer both questions we have to go back to the early 1790s.

One of the first things John Graves Simcoe did when he arrived from Britain to administer to the needs of the new Province of Upper Canada (Ontario) was to look for a place where his men could build warships. There was no doubt in Simcoe's mind that these ships would be needed to protect against an invasion by American forces. Having fought for the English in the recent Revolutionary War, he was convinced that the victorious Americans were more eager than ever to overrun Britain's colonies in North America. Simcoe needed those ships to defend against this threat.

After surveying the north shore of Lake Ontario, he selected what we now know as Toronto Harbour as the place to establish a shipyard. The location was perfect for his needs. With the Toronto Islands still a peninsula, connected at their east end to the mainland by a narrow isthmus (the Eastern Gap wasn't created until 1858 when a monster storm breached the isthmus), the only way an invader could attack the shipyard, and the small community that had been established nearby, was to sail a fleet through the only entrance that existed back then—a narrow channel at the west end of the harbour.

This configuration made defence of the harbour easy. Simcoe would build fortifications on the water's edge north of the channel, with cannons aimed south toward the channel. Over on the peninsula he constructed a wooden blockhouse, also aiming its cannon at the channel. Any vessel attempting to enter the harbour would be blasted to pieces from both sides. The mainland fortification evolved into what we now know as Fort York, while that old blockhouse remains only in the name of Blockhouse Bay located opposite the Hanlan's Point ferry dock.

Although the invasion anticipated by Simcoe didn't materialize during his tenure as lieutenant governor, war did break out some years later. One of the major battles of the War of 1812 took place in the spring of 1813 when American forces overran the fort at York (soon to be renamed Toronto) and occupied the town for several days. This battle, and other clashes throughout the province during the war, did much to define Upper Canadians as a people not to be messed with.

In 1934, Toronto's centennial year, the fortification, now called Fort York, was restored with a great deal of civic pride. For the next couple of decades the fort was one of the city's most popular attractions. This pride was severely tested in the late 1950s as work progressed on the elevated portion of the new Lakeshore Expressway (soon renamed the Gardiner Expressway). Officials wanted to put the expressway right over the fort. However, many history-minded citizens refused to accept that proposition, saying such a structure would desecrate both the fort and the nearby military cemetery.

In an attempt to placate those opposed to an ugly, noisy highway over the ancient fort, an offer was made in the spring of 1958 to move the historic site, lock, stock, and blockhouses, to Coronation Park, a grass-and-treed area on the water's edge south of Princes' Gate.

Metro Chairman Fred Gardiner, perhaps forgetting his early Toronto history and the fact that years of dumping landfill had removed the fort from its waterside location, went as far as to suggest that it would be nice to have the fort back on the water's edge where it belonged. But concerned Torontonians would have nothing to do with his suggestion. Eventually, the highway designers were ordered to rework the right-of-way, and as a result, the old fort stayed put and the new highway was moved. Make that a "save" for heritage.

This 1961 aerial view looks down on the intersection of Bathurst Street and Lake Shore Boulevard. The old Maple Leaf Stadium is at the bottom, while the new Lakeshore (soon to be Gardiner) Expressway skirts the ramparts of historic Fort York.

Doing Time in T.O.

In the spring of 2006 a ceremony sponsored by the Riverdale Historical Society—an organization established in late 1999 to discover, preserve, and promote the history of Riverdale—was held, at which time a Heritage Toronto commemorative plaque was unveiled in front of the famous, or should I say infamous, Don Jail.

Riverdale is defined as the area bounded by Lake Ontario to the south, Pape and Danforth avenues to the east and north respectively, and the Don River to the west. Riverdale, known in former days as Riverside, was the location of numerous farms, many of which supplied provisions to the earliest settlers in the Town of York. One of those farms was owned by John Scadding, who had managed John Graves Simcoe's estate back in England. When Simcoe was ordered to take charge of the newly created Province of Upper Canada, Scadding agreed to accompany him and was subsequently granted a parcel of land on the east bank of the Don River, a property bounded on the south, east, and north by today's Queen Street, Broadview Avenue, and Danforth Avenue.

Incidentally, one of the many structures Scadding built on his farm was a small cabin that was moved to the Canadian National Exhibition grounds in 1879. Under the care of the York Pioneers, Scadding Cabin continues to serve as a reminder of Toronto's past.

In 1856, 120 acres at the north end of the Scadding farm were sold to the city as the site of a House of Industry and Refuge (the forerunner of today's Bridgepoint health complex), an industrial farm, and a jail that would serve the city's troublemakers as well as those from the surrounding County of York.

The new jail was designed by prominent city architect William Thomas, whose earlier works, St. Michael's Cathedral and St. Lawrence Hall, had already earned distinction as civic landmarks. While work on the new jail actually began in 1859, numerous delays meant its first "guests" weren't welcomed inside for another five years.

For the next 113 years the Don Jail was a stopover for thousands, with many of the 70 or so convicted of murder and lacking next-of-kin finding a permanent home in

This Heritage Toronto plaque was unveiled in 2006 on the grounds of historic Don Jail.

the small graveyard behind the hulking building. Arguably the best known of its many inmates were several members of Edwin Alonzo Boyd's gang of bank robbers, two of whom, Steve Suchan and Lennie Jackson, were hanged for the murder of a Toronto police officer. A close second in the race for notoriety (and the answer to a favourite trivia question) would be Arthur Lucas and Ronald Turpin, who together have the distinction of being the last people hanged in Canada, a deed that took place on December 11, 1962.

The Don Jail, which was closed in 1977 (the Toronto Jail next door is still in business), is now administered by Bridgepoint Health. Plans call for the historic building to be sympathetically renovated for community use.

Winged Victory is seen high atop the Princes' Gates as a police officer waves a "winged" 1959 Buick through the entrance.

Fanciful Flights

Held for the first time in the fall of 1879, what we know today as the Canadian National Exhibition was originally called the Toronto Industrial Exhibition and was organized to protest the Provincial Agricultural and Arts Association's refusal to designate Ontario's capital city as the permanent home of the association's annual fair.

And so while the Agricultural and Arts people went ahead and held their event in Ottawa in 1879, Toronto officials, led by city politician and lumber merchant John J. Withrow, put together the first edition of what would become the forerunner of today's CNE.

As the fair grew in popularity, it became necessary to expand the site. One of the first such expansions took in property west of Dufferin Street and south of the railway tracks down to the old waterfront. It was on this land that the International, British Governments and, in 1926, Ontario Government buildings were constructed. The first mentioned was destroyed by fire in 1974, while the last two are home to today's Medieval Times Dinner and Tournament and Liberty Grand Entertainment Complex respectively.

To coincide with the expansion of the CNE grounds, a new entrance was built in 1910 to replace the old wooden structure located on the east side of Dufferin Street just south of the tracks. The flamboyant new entrance was called the Dufferin Memorial Gate. Years later, when planners were working on the route of the Gardiner Expressway, they determined that the old gate had to go. It was replaced by today's modern, though less flashy, entrance.

When it came time to expand and develop the east end of the grounds, officials decided that one of the key components, in addition to a couple of new buildings (Electrical and Engineering, demolished in 1974, and Automotive), would also be a magnificent new entrance. With the 60th anniversary of the coming together of the first four Canadian provinces approaching, it was felt that Diamond Jubilee of Confederation Gate would be the perfect name for the new entrance. As part of the design, the architects of the gate, Chapman and Oxley, chose to emulate a likeness of *Nike of Samothrace*, a Greek sculpture discovered in 1863 and now on display in Paris's Louvre, to stand high atop the central entranceway.

The statue of *Winged Victory*, also known as *Nike of Samothrace*, is on display at the Louvre in Paris.

Sculpted by the talented artist Charles McKechnie (1865–1935), Toronto's version of the Greek sculpture, frequently referred to as "The Angel," was said to be a female representation of the young Canadian nation of 1927 proudly standing in her "ship of state" sailing confidently into a future full of hope and progress.

Over the years, the sculpted figure fell victim to icy spray off the lake and numerous lightning strikes and was replaced in 1987 with a glass-reinforced polymer plastic copy created by Summit Restoration.

Mi Casa Loma

Sometime ago it was my pleasure to accompany a group of women from Kansas as they toured Toronto. During our time together, I asked one of the ladies what had prompted the group to select this city as their destination. Was it the theatres, the restaurants, the shopping?

Her answer took me somewhat by surprise. As young girls growing up in the U.S. Midwest, many of them had heard about a fairy-tale castle in a far-off place called Toronto. They were too young even to know what or where this thing called Toronto was; however, each of them knew that someday they would visit that castle.

Years later, when the same group got together to plan a special holiday, the consensus was that they would visit the castle they all remembered reading about as kids. That's why they were in Toronto and why their first visit was not to a show, a shopping centre, or a restaurant, but to Casa Loma.

Of course, they were curious just who would build such an unusual structure and why. The first part of the question was easy to answer. It was built by a truly unique Canadian, Sir Henry Pellatt, who was born in Kingston, Canada West (Ontario), in 1859, and passed away in a Toronto suburb on March 8, 1939.

When still a young man, Henry entered his father's brokerage business and was soon on his way to amassing a fortune through the art of knowing when to buy and when to sell a wide variety of stocks and bonds. His successes in buying and selling huge amounts of land in the still sparsely settled areas of western Canada along the new Canadian Pacific Railway's right-of-way added to his riches, as did his venture into the wonderful new world of electricity.

As to why he built his Toronto residence, which he called Casa Loma after the piece of property on which it would be erected, one only has to look at Sir Henry's

Sir Henry Pellatt gazes at a portrait of himself as a young man.

competitive nature. When some of his well-heeled contemporaries began building their mansions on the escarpment that runs across the top of the city just north of Davenport Road, it was part of Sir Henry's temperament to "one-up" each and every one of them.

The Eaton family had its Ardwold (from the Gaelic "high green hill" and located on the east side of Spadina Road south of the St. Clair Avenue intersection), while the piano-building Nordheimers lived in a place a little farther to the west called Glen Edyth (so named in recognition of the nearby glen and Samuel's young bride, Edith). On the east side of the Avenue Road hill stood the late Senator Macdonald's Oaklands, a stately mansion that today is part of De La Salle School. When Sir Henry was contemplating his castle, Oaklands belonged to Miss McCormick, daughter of Cyrus McCormick, inventor of a revolutionary reaper.

But most of all, Pellatt wanted to build a bigger and more prestigious mansion than Benvenuto, the place his friend Sir William Mackenzie called home. It was Mackenzie with whom Pellatt had many financial dealings, including the innovative scheme to establish the Electrical Development Company (EDC) and bring electricity generated at Niagara Falls to Toronto. They accomplished their goal long before the provincial government got into the "power for the people" business (a belief Ontario recently abandoned). Mackenzie's magnificent Benvenuto was located on the west side of the Avenue Road hill (on a site now occupied by an apartment complex, the wall of which still exists) and had been built in 1888 by Simeon Janes, the real estate entrepreneur who developed what we now know as the Annex.

One way for Sir Henry to outdo his business allies and foes alike was to build something unique. Having been impressed by the many castles he had visited on tours throughout England, Scotland, and France, Sir Henry—who by 1911, when work on the castle began, had a personal worth of many millions—had his architect friend, E.J. Lennox, design a castle just for him. Lennox had recently designed the mammoth EDC Generating Station at Niagara Falls and was still trying to get paid for his work on an earlier commission, a place we now know as "Old" City Hall.

More than two years and $3.5 million later, the Pellatts moved in to their new home, which everyone viewed with awe. What we now call "market value reassessment" forced them to move out of Casa Loma just a decade later, and there were calls to tear it down.

Today the castle, which is owned by the City of Toronto, is operated by the Kiwanis Club of Casa Loma.

Milestones in Medicine

Our community is blessed with many fine hospitals. One of the oldest and busiest is St. Michael's, which today is located in the heart of Toronto on Queen Street East between Victoria and Bond streets. But when St. Mike's first opened its doors in 1892 it occupied a building located on the west side of Bond Street just north of Queen that had originally been built as a Baptist church. In more recent years it had been converted for the Sisters of St. Joseph for use as a boarding house for working mothers. In the early 1890s, Toronto was suffering through a serious diphtheria epidemic. Without sufficient help to assist those afflicted, the medical officer of health sent out a plea for aid. The sisters, who had arrived in Toronto 40 years earlier in response to a request for assistance during a typhoid epidemic, responded quickly, converting the Bond Street boarding house into an infirmary where diphtheria victims could be treated. Soon the tiny building was being referred to as St. Michael's Hospital.

Over the years the hospital expanded through the construction of new buildings on the Queen and Bond corner until today St. Mike's covers the entire block, with additional hospital facilities nearby.

Numerous medical milestones have been achieved by staff of this remarkable hospital. For instance, St. Mike's was the site of one of the first blood transfusions in Canada (1917) and where one of the first open-heart operations in the province was performed (1958). It was also the first hospital in the country to perform a successful heart transplant (1968) and the first in the world to successfully transplant a sciatic nerve (1988).

An interesting feature of the hospital is the use of a statue of its namesake, St. Michael, as the hospital's "spokesperson." The statue of the archangel is featured in a variety of ways, including a rendition on the giant billboard on the west wall of the hospital. In 1997, when the statue, which has been on display inside the Bond Street entrance for many years, was moved to a new location in the new Victoria Street wing, someone noticed the word *Pietasantra* carved on the its back. This term indicated that the marble from which this figure was carved was from the same quarry as the one that supplied the material for Michelangelo's famous sculpture *Pieta*. Just how the statue of St. Michael got to be in our city is a mystery, as is the name of the sculptor and when the work was created. On the other hand, how the work got to the hospital is easy to explain. It seems the sisters saw it in the window of a Queen Street pawnbroker, and after some negotiating, bought it for $49—money they had raised by collecting and selling old newspapers.

An early twentieth-century postcard view looks east on Queen Street to Victoria Street.

Today, in the same view of Queen and Victoria streets, St. Michael's Hospital dominates the scene.

7

Toronto Then and Now

On the Banks of the Don

One of the perks associated with writing a column is getting letters from readers that contain additional information relative to a story I've written. Even better is when the letter is accompanied by an old photograph or postcard.

An example of this latter occurrence arrived soon after the appearance of my January 1, 2006, column entitled "Postcards of the Past." In the envelope was a pair of "before and after" postcards of a group taking advantage of the snow-covered hills somewhere, the reader thought, in Toronto. The cards, which were in his late grandmother's collection, were dated March 1, 1913.

In addition, there were two names printed on the reverse of each card, "Brightling, 179 Roselawn" and "G.L. Riches, Photographer and Publisher, Brockville, Ontario." Perusal of the city directory for 1913 disclosed that Mr. William H. Brightling was a photographer and was obviously chosen to photograph the group's outing, while a call to the Brockville Library revealed Mr. Riches was in the business of printing postcards for members of the general public.

The clue to where the photos were taken is the small two-storey structure in the left background of the first card. It's the old Swiss Cottage, a hospital in which victims of highly infectious diseases such as smallpox and scarlet fever could be isolated during treatment. In

This happy group is set for a fast run down the snow-covered slopes at Toronto's Riverdale Park in 1913.

Ooops! A photogenic spill. Keen eyes will see there are two more people in this photo than in the picture above.

fact, the building was also known by the rather unsympathetic title of Isolation Hospital. Constructed in 1906 at a cost of $5,000, it was built in what the newspapers of the day described as "the picturesque Swiss-style." As to its location, let me quote from the *Evening Telegram*: "The city's new Swiss Cottage is bosomed in the precipitous cliffs that overlook the eastern banks of the Don. Looked at from the river flats [incidentally, the vantage point from which this photo was taken], it occupies a commanding height yet behind and beside it to a height of 40 feet above it rise the steep banks of the Don."

In today's terms that little hospital would have been located to the north of the Don Jail and the modern Bridgepoint Health (formerly Riverdale Hospital), with the modern Broadview Avenue up and over the hill in the background. When more modern isolation facilities were eventually built, the Swiss Cottage was purposely burned to the ground by the city's fire department.

Capsule Moment

The older of the two photos accompanying this story might appear at first glance to be simply a view of a Toronto street intersection, in this case the one at King Street and University Avenue as it looked in 1952. But as with most old pictures there's a lot more in the photo than first meets the eye. For instance, a Hoskin Coach Lines bus in "charter" service can be seen turning north on University from King. Where was it going? Where had it been? Who was onboard? And who was Hoskin, anyway? Questions. Questions.

The PCC streetcar in the same view, headed east on the King route, was built at the St. Louis Car Company's factory in St. Louis, Missouri, in 1942, with final fitting-out completed at the Canadian Car and Foundry factory in Montreal. In the early 1970s this car and nine other similar TTC vehicles would be sold to Tampico, Mexico, where they would operate alongside additional second-hand PCCs obtained from other American cities. All streetcar operations in that Mexican city ended in 1974.

Visible in the background of the 1952 photo are three of the city's most prominent buildings of the day. At the extreme right is the 1931 Bank of Commerce, described as the tallest building in what was still proudly identified as the British Commonwealth. Across King Street at number 80 is the *Daily Star*'s building, and nearby, at the northeast corner of York Street, is the art deco–style home of the *Globe*

Looking east on King Street to University Avenue in 1952.

A similar view in 2005.

and Mail. Note also that the cost to park in the empty lot at the King and University corner is 25 cents an hour. Japanese cars have yet to appear on the city streets, but two English ones appear prominently. And over in the parking lot is a Studebaker. Remember them?

In the modern-day photo a Canadian Light Rail Vehicle maintains the tradition of streetcars on the King route (the first horse-drawn car appeared in 1874) as it glides by the towering Sun Life Centre, which opened in 1984.

On the Wharf

One of the most famous views of Old Toronto is W.H. Bartlett's *The Fish Market*, shown here and contrasted (approximately) with a modern-day view. Bartlett's work appears on notepaper, postcards, dinner plates, and in my household on a kitchen place mat. In most present-day instances the view is reproduced in colour, though the original sketch—which appeared in the book *Canadian Scenery*, an extremely rare two-volume work by Nathaniel Parker Willis published in 1842— was printed in black and white. Therefore, whenever Bartlett's sketches appear in colour, those hues are actually the creation of a retouching artist's imagination.

William Bartlett was born in Kentish Town, London, England, in 1809. The talented young man travelled extensively throughout Europe, the Middle East, and North America—all the while sketching what he saw. Many of his works were subsequently used to illustrate a large number of travel books, one of which was Willis's informative *Canadian Scenery*. Although published in 1842, the views, including the two in the book that depict Toronto, were actually done during Bartlett's visit, which many believe actually occurred four years earlier in 1838. If that assumption is correct, then the city he sketched would only have been in existence for a mere four years.

The Fish Market by English artist W.H. Bartlett.

The view in *The Fish Market* looks west along the "front" road of the city, thus the thoroughfare's official name of Front Street. As you can see, there were no buildings along the south side of Front during Bartlett's visit, or for many years after, for that matter. It wasn't until the value of downtown property began to increase that landfill was used to extend the shoreline into the harbour—and that didn't occur for many more years. Today that old shoreline is still noticeable as a gradient south of Front Street on many of the north-south thoroughfares in the city's core.

If you examine Bartlett's print closely, you'll notice that the structure to the left is a storage building at the end of Cooper's Wharf. This wharf was one of several that jutted into the harbour; Cooper's was at the foot of Church Street. In the centre of the picture is a building that, because of its shape, wedged as it was between the convergence of Front and Wellington streets at Church, and the fact that it was built out of wood, was popularly known as the Coffin Block. For many years it was the city terminal for William Weller's popular stagecoach company, which operated

Looking west on Front Street at Church Street in the early 1970s, with the CN Tower under construction beyond the Gooderham (Flatiron) Building.

numerous horse-drawn conveyances between Toronto, Hamilton, Holland Landing, and Kingston.

In the early 1890s the old, now-dilapidated structure was torn down and the present Gooderham Building, seen in this view from the early 1970s, was erected on the site.

City at the Crossroads

Recently, Bazis International Inc. revealed that it plans to erect a towering 80-floor retail/condominium/hotel at the southeast corner of Yonge and Bloor streets. This massive project will be known as 1 Bloor East.

Founded in 1991, Bazis International originated in the Republic of Kazakhstan, a sprawling country covering just over a million square miles in Central Asia. Kazakhstan has a population of more than seven million, and its capital city is Astana, population 600,000. The company has a workforce of more than 13,000 employees and has designed and built a wide variety of residential communities, office towers, government buildings, hotels, theatres, malls, and industrial complexes. The 1 Bloor East project is the company's second in Toronto, the first being the Crystal Blu condominium currently under construction on nearby Balmuto Street.

The illustration in this column shows an artist's concept of what the Yonge and Bloor project will look like upon completion. In the photograph, which looks east on Bloor across Yonge, we can see how the corner appeared in 1953. A streetcar on the Bloor-Danforth route trundles through the intersection in the foreground. Streetcars continued to operate on Yonge until the route ended with the inauguration of the Yonge subway a few months after this picture was taken. Visible in the distance is the Bloor streetcar loading platform. The Bloor streetcars in this part of town were retired when the first section of the Bloor-Danforth subway opened for business in 1966.

Also evident in the distance is the Towne Cinema, which at the time featured a somewhat higher class of films. The church tower belongs to Westminster Central United, a structure that was demolished shortly after this photo was snapped. Also in the view is Chez Moi Restaurant. On the north side of Bloor is the Royal Bank Building and apartments. This site is now occupied by an unimaginative office block.

Yonge Street recognizes Sir George Yonge, a friend of city founder John Graves Simcoe and a fellow politician in the British Parliament. He was born in 1731 and died at 81, having held such British positions as secretary of war, master of the mint, and lastly, governor of Cape Colony in Africa. In his spare time Yonge studied the art of Roman road-building.

Joseph Bloor was born in Staffordshire, England, in 1789. He arrived in the Town of York in 1818 or 1819.

An artist's sketch of the 1 Bloor East project. (Courtesy Bazis International Inc.)

Bloor Street looking east from Yonge Street in 1953. The 1 Bloor East project will be situated on the corner behind the streetcar.

Bloor ran a hotel near the St. Lawrence Market before relocating to the countryside north of town, where he established a brewery north and east of today's Yonge and Bloor intersection. With his neighbour William Jarvis, Bloor began dabbling in land development in an area that is now part of fashionable Yorkville. Bloor built a substantial residence on what was simply known as the First Concession, a thoroughfare that eventually took on his surname.

Pride of Ownership

Spadina Hotel at the corner of Spadina Avenue and King Street circa 1968.

Located at the northwest corner of the "ancient" Spadina and King intersection is a former hotel that's been a Toronto landmark for more than 130 years. In 1997 the old building got a new lease on life, and while it still serves the travelling public, its customers no longer arrive by horse and wagon with a selection of suitcases in hand as they did when the place first opened as the Richardson House in 1875. Today guests make their way by foot and streetcar carrying packs on their backs to the appropriately named Global Village Backpackers Hostel, the largest of its kind in the city. It offers 190 beds, pleasant surroundings, friendly staff, and an economical spot to stay while exploring our city.

During the old building's long history, it has carried more than just the Richardson House and Global Village Backpackers names on its marquee. In fact, in 1906, just 19 years after the original owner Samuel Richardson added the second of two substantial additions to his hotel—both of which are plainly visible to the north of the original three-storey structure—the business was purchased by Robert Falconer and soon bore the name Hotel Falconer. The next owner, Charlie Zeigler, took over proprietorship in 1914, and for three years the place was known as Zeigler's Hotel. Then another owner, J.A. Johnson, renamed the business once again, this time with a title that many people will remember— or after some time in the Cabana Room, not remember—the Spadina Hotel.

The old "Spad" will spark fond memories for many of its customers. In addition, the place has an interesting connection with the *Toronto Sun* for, as author Jean Sonmor recounts in her fascinating book *The Little Paper That Grew*, it was at the hotel bar that on one day in the mid-1960s Johnny Bassett, son of the *Telegram* publisher, and Doug Creighton, the newspaper's sports editor, talked about the creation of a morning tabloid to take the place of the venerable old paper should the inconceivable happen and the *Tely* succumb to its rival, the *Toronto Star*.

Over the next few years the idea of a morning tabloid for the city surfaced several more times, but nothing actually happened. That is until late October 1971 when the *Telegram* breathed its last and quietly folded. First published in 1876, the unthinkable had happened— the good, old *Tely* was no more.

Just two days later, November 1, 1971, that idea of a new morning paper that had been bandied about in the Spadina Hotel by Doug and Johnny a half-decade earlier came to pass and the *Toronto Sun* was born.

The same view today. The old hotel is now the site of a popular hostel operated by Global Village Backpackers. (Photo courtesy Matt Wyatt)

FILEY *Fact*

One of Toronto's first hotels was Jordan's York City Hotel. It opened in 1801 on King Street East on a site that the *Toronto Sun* building occupies today. The place was popular not only for meals and overnight stays, but it also served as the home of the Upper Canada Parliament after the destruction of the original Parliament Buildings during the occupation of the community by American forces in 1813 in the War of 1812.

Facelift for Toronto's Central Piazza

I had a note from reader Bill Sandford asking if, with all the talk about revitalizing Nathan Phillips Square, I had any photos of what the area looked like before New City Hall was built. Yes, Bill, I do, and an aerial view of the site taken in 1947 accompanies this column. The street at the bottom of the picture is Queen, with the Manning Chambers Building at the Bay corner to the extreme right. North of it is Shea's Hippodrome, one of Toronto's most popular movie palaces. When it opened in 1917, Bay was still known as Terauley Street. At the top left is the Armouries on University Avenue, and to the right of it is the imposing Registry Building. A variety of hotels and restaurants line Chestnut Street in what was Toronto's original Chinatown.

Nathan Phillips Square was named in honour of "Nate" Phillips, who was first elected to City Council in 1924. He continued to serve as an alderman until elected mayor in 1955, holding that position until 1962. While the idea of a new municipal building to replace Old City Hall was rejected several times, it was Nate's persistence that finally resulted in the construction of Toronto's present City Hall. Soon after construction began in 1961, City Council voted to name the public space in front of architect Viljo Revell's masterpiece for the man who was proud to be known as the "mayor of all the people." By the way, the plan to revitalize Nathan Phillips Square is budgeted at $40 million, $10 million more than the cost of New City Hall itself.

This aerial view, taken in 1947, shows the area where Nathan Phillips Square is now. At the top left of the photo are the Armouries and the Registry Building, both since demolished.

Nathan Phillips Square and Toronto's New City Hall a few months prior to the official opening in September 1965.

Historic Home on the Move

It's hard for me to believe that I sat with Yarmila, my wife of a little more than three years at the time (and yes, we're still together), on the roof of the former Sun Life Building at University Avenue and Richmond Street in 1972 and watched with awe as an old house inched its way along Adelaide Street (the wrong way, I might add), then north on University. The structure that was slowly creeping past our vantage point was historic Campbell House on its way to a new site at the northwest corner of the Queen Street intersection. Originally destined for demolition, the house is one of the city's few true landmarks to make it into the twenty-first century.

William Campbell was born in Scotland in 1758 and came to North America to fight for Great Britain during the American Revolutionary War. At the end of the war he moved to Nova Scotia where he studied and practised law. His career was

Campbell House was erected on Duke Street (now Adelaide Street East) at the top of Frederick Street in 1822 and moved to its present location at the northwest corner of University Avenue and Queen Street exactly 150 years later. Here it sits at its original location.

undistinguished, and he frequently clashed with others in the profession. Campbell was eager to move on, and in 1811 he made his way to Upper Canada. Arriving in York, he was given a judge-ship along with a town lot on Duke Street in the heart of the old town where, in 1822, he built a substantial residence. Incidentally, Duke was one of the original thoroughfares in York and like many others was named to honour British royalty. The name was derived from the Duke of York, whose first name, Freder-ick, became the name of the street that led from Campbell's house south to the harbour. Although this latter street is still there, it was cut off from the waterfront long ago. Duke Street retained its name until the mid-twentieth century when traffic engineers connected it with Adelaide Street to the west of Jarvis Street and eliminated the name Duke. Something similar happened to the original Duchess Street (one street north of old Duke), which was connected with Richmond and is now known by the latter name.

Sir William was appointed chief justice of Upper Canada in 1825, but only four years later ill health forced him to retire. Soon after his retirement, word was received that he had been knighted. Sir William Campbell died in his house in 1834, the same year the town was elevated to city status and was given back its original name of Toronto.

Over the following years, Campbell's residence was used for a variety of purposes, including a manufactory for horseshoe nails, an elevator factory, a storehouse for electrical supplies, and finally as a warehouse associated with a greeting card com-pany. It was in this last guise that the fast-deteriorating building, by now one of the oldest in the rapidly growing modern city, was given last rites. Until, that is, a group of lawyers who had recently established themselves under the title of The Advocates' Society agreed to consider the possibility of preserving the chief justice's house.

Early in 1969 the owners of the old house offered to sell it to the society for $1, provided it was moved to another location. Over the next two years a newly formed organization, the Sir William Campbell Foundation, expedited fundraising efforts while at the same time plans continued to find a place to relocate the ancient structure. All this work came to a head on March 31, 1972 (Good Friday), when the project to move the 300-ton building got underway. Thousands watched as the structure made its way from the old town to its new site at the northwest corner of Queen and University. Months of restoration and refurbishment followed, and on June 28, 1974, Campbell House was officially opened by the Queen Mother.

Today the house is one of the many attractions that remind us of Toronto's past.

Today Canada Life towers over the historic house.

Once Around the Park

One of the most imposing sights in Toronto is that of the Parliament Buildings of Ontario as seen from the busy University Avenue–College Street intersection. Although the buildings are called Queen's Park by most people, that term is actually the name of the large park in which the structure was erected in the early 1890s. It was given the name "the Queen's Park" by Edward, the Prince of Wales, Queen Victoria's eldest son, during a huge public ceremony held on September 11, 1860.

Actually, the dedication service was planned for the previous Saturday, but heavy rains put an end to that idea. Since the young prince was going to be in town for a few more days, the event was rescheduled for the following Tuesday. While that day started off nicely, by the time the prince arrived, it was raining heavily once again.

It was now or never, though, so with Edward protected under a canopy, the ceremony went ahead. However, before the park was dedicated in his mother's honour, the prince was asked to say a few words at the laying of the foundation stone on which a grand statue of his mother would eventually be placed. The location

The thoroughfare called Queen's Park looking north from the park of the same name, circa 1930. In the distance is the Queen's Park Plaza Hotel that, because of a number of financial and construction-related issues, was still six years away from opening. Today the hotel is known as the Park Hyatt. To the extreme right is the recently completed Emmanuel College.

A similar view in 2007. Queen's Park, as well as several other city thoroughfares, was widened during the Great Depression in an effort to put as many people to work as possible.

of her monument was to be at the extreme south end of the park, a site now occupied by a statue that honours Sir John A. Macdonald.

While the pedestal was "well and truly laid" by her son, 10 years passed before the new statue of the queen arrived. But now there was another problem: there wasn't enough money to pay for it, so back to England it went.

Then, with sentiment running high after Victoria's death in 1901, the statue idea was revived and enough money was raised to bring the statue back to Toronto. But now Sir John's monument (erected in 1894) was in the way. As a result, Queen Victoria was relegated to a less grand location under the trees west of the main entrance to the Parliament Buildings.

As for the name of the park, prior to the prince's visit in September 1860, it had been known simply as University Park, an obvious title since it contained approximately 166 acres of land that was sold by several prominent landowners to the newly established King's College, the forerunner of today's University of Toronto. Then, in 1859, the university leased the park to the city for 999 years at $6,000 per annum with the proviso that a portion of it be reserved for new parliament buildings.

The Legislative Buildings of Ontario at the top of University Avenue were officially opened by the lieutenant governor of the day, George Kirkpatrick, on April 4, 1893.

Streetcars on Track

Public transit in Toronto took a short but important step forward when the first section of the new St. Clair streetcar right-of-way opened in 2007. Now the streetcars, and all the passengers onboard, have clear sailing between the Yonge and St. Clair West subway stations. Work to clear the track all the way to Keele Street continues.

Interestingly, when streetcars first appeared on St. Clair on August 25, 1913, they operated along a right-of-way that kept them separated from other traffic on the street. That condition remained until the last portion of this centre-of-the-street reservation was removed in 1935.

Over the following years traffic along St. Clair increased and various attempts were made to give the St. Clair cars priority. Nothing worked, and it was decided to seek permission to revive the idea of a centre-of-the-street streetcar right-of-way. City Council gave its go-ahead to proceed with the preferred design concept on October 1, 2004, followed eight months later by provincial environmental approval. Construction began September 22, 2005, only to be blocked less than two months later by legal action prompted by a local citizens' group. This decision was eventually overturned and work resumed on the Yonge Street to Vaughan Road stretch in the summer of 2006. This section opened on February 18, 2007.

The fact that it took so long to get the first phase of this transit improvement project is typical of the roadblocks that have faced many of the attempts to improve

FILEY *Fact*

One of the city's true landmarks is the massive structure that spans the valley of the Don River and connects Bloor Street at Sherbourne with "the Danforth." And while most people call it the Bloor Street Viaduct, its official name is the Prince Edward Viaduct. That title was selected by City Council on September 3, 1919, to honour Edward, the Prince of Wales, whose visit to the city a week earlier had been a resounding success. He's also one of the "princes" in the term Princes' Gates. (The other was Prince George, the Duke of Kent.) While streetcars along Bloor and the Danforth have been replaced by trains on the east-west subway, 504 King and 505 Dundas streetcars still cross Danforth Avenue east of the bridge.

transportation in and around Toronto. A case in point: when the first section of the Yonge subway, Union Station to Eglinton, finally got rolling on March 30, 1954, nearly four and a half decades had passed since the idea of burrowing underground was first promoted as a way to alleviate the ever-increasing traffic congestion clogging the city's streets. One of those promoters was James Grand, the founder of the pioneer Grand & Toy stationery firm. In the 1910 edition of his company's in-house magazine *Grand*, he wrote the following: "Toronto will soon round out the half-million mark in population and better transportation facilities will be an absolute necessity. Why not go ahead with the tunnel scheme and be ready in advance?"

Prophetic perhaps, but nothing further happened. The subway idea was revived in 1912 when the question of building one appeared on that year's municipal ballot. The wording was: "Will you authorize the City Council to spend the sum of $5,386,870 for an underground railway from the corner of Bay and Front Street, northerly to the corner of St. Clair Avenue and Yonge Street?"

Not surprisingly, the electorate regarded that amount of money as far too much for the young city to swallow, and the idea of a subway was soundly defeated. Then came the Great War, and any ideas related to public transit seemed pretty

Looking west along St. Clair Avenue across Avenue Road in 1911. While streetcars were operating up to the corner from downtown, service on St. Clair is still a couple of years in the future.

insignificant as the world appeared to be coming apart.

The next time the idea of a subway came forward was early in the Great Depression when its construction was suggested as a way of putting 3,000 unemployed people to work digging a 20-foot-deep trench down Yonge Street from Ramsden Park to Front Street through which streetcars could run. Again nothing happened.

In 1942, realizing the crunch that would come when the Second World War was finally over, the Toronto Transit Commission established a Rapid Transit Department. The citizens, too, had seen the light, and in the municipal election of 1946 they voted overwhelmingly to build a subway. Work began on September 8, 1949, and on March 30, 1954, the Yonge subway, Canada's first, was officially opened.

Let's see, it took nearly 55 months to build the 4.6 miles of what was Toronto's first subway. It took 17 months to build a little more than a mile of above-ground streetcar right-of-way. Nothing comes easy these days.

Looking west along St. Clair Avenue toward Avenue Road in 2007. After months of bickering, construction finally got underway in earnest in mid-2006 with the first phase of the project opening on February 18, 2007.

8

Toronto on the Move

Across the Bay

On June 18, 1910, the newest vessel to join the lengthy list of ferry boats serving the Toronto Islands entered the water in the slip adjacent to the busy Polson Iron Works shipyard at the foot of Sherbourne Street. Built for the Toronto Ferry Company (TFC), a privately owned enterprise that had been granted a monopoly in 1890 by the city to provide cross-bay service, the still unnamed craft was the finest, most modern that money (well, at least $75,000 worth) could buy.

The new vessel was double-ended and was powered by a double-compound steam engine connected to twin side paddles that allowed the craft to "race" across the bay at a top speed of 10 miles per hour (8.7 knots).

The double-ended feature was important because the vessel would spend most of its time during the spring, summer, and fall ferrying thousands of baseball fans to and from the large stadium at Hanlan's Point. Here they would cheer on their beloved Maple Leafs as they challenged other teams in the International League, an association of baseball teams one level below the majors playing south of the border. Being double-ended meant the craft could load and unload at both ends without having to turn the vessel in mid-bay, a manoeuvre that would obviously delay getting there to witness that all-important first pitch.

Actually, the necessity of a new boat became apparent not long after the company put *Blue Bell*, anther double-ender, on the Hanlan's Point run in 1906. As the team became more and more popular (the club won the league championship in 1907), the cross-bay traffic increased and this, combined with a new 18,000-seat concrete stadium built to replace the antiquated wooden stand destroyed by fire on August 10, 1909, resulted in the company placing an order for a second boat of similar dimensions with the Polson Iron Works people.

Although this new craft would be christened *Trillium*, that name wasn't the company's first choice. To be sure, the company wanted to maintain the long-standing tradition of naming its boats after flowers as it had with *Blue Bell* and two earlier, smaller vessels, *Mayflower* and *Primrose*. In fact, the first thought was to name the craft *Arbutus* (a species of flower also known as the mayflower), but unfortunately (or, in retrospect, fortunately) that name had already been given to another vessel. So another choice was put forward. This time it was *Hawthorne*, but again the name was already being used. They then tried *Golden Rod*. Again no luck. Try again. Finally, and perhaps out of desperation, *Trillium* was put forward, and after a thorough search in the official registry books, that name was accepted. *Trillium* it would be.

And thus it was when the still-unfinished hull and superstructure slid sideways into the Polson slip on June 18, 1910, the sturdy craft finally had a name. Two weeks later the boat, now fitted out and with the name *Trillium* proudly emblazoned on its twin paddle boxes, entered service on Toronto Bay.

For the next 47 years *Trillium* safely carried thousands to and from the Toronto Islands, initially under the ownership of the TFC and later the Toronto Transit Commission. Then, with a dramatic drop in the number of visitors to the islands and the trio of diesel ferry boats (*Inglis, McBride,* and *Rennie*) now up to the task, both *Blue Bell* and *Trillium* were cast aside. While *Blue Bell* was eventually scrapped, a kinder fate awaited *Trillium* when on November 13, 1973, Metro Toronto politicians authorized the expenditure of $950,000 to return the historic vessel to service.

For the next two years, and under the watchful eye of Project Director Gordon Champion, *Trillium* was primped and prodded at Herb Fraser's shipyard in Port Colborne, Ontario. On November 7, 1975, the vessel returned to fog-shrouded Toronto Bay. The following May *Trillium* was back in service.

The paddle steamer *Trillium*, circa 1920.

Toronto Islands ferry *Trillium* enters the Welland Canal's Lock 7 as it returns home after a mandatory hull inspection. (Photo courtesy Yarmila Filey)

A Real-life Ferry Tale

Back in the early years of the twentieth century a wide variety of passenger boats operated between the Port of Toronto and other ports on both the Canadian and American sides of Lake Ontario. These vessels carried names such as SS *Turbinia*, SS *Kingston*, SS *Toronto*, and SS *Cayuga*, and over the years they carried thousands to and from places such as Lewiston in New York State and Queenston, Hamilton, Kingston, and Brockville on this side of the border. In fact, one of the most popular destinations for Torontonians was the quaint U.S. town of Charlotte at the mouth of the Genesee River. Nearby was Ontario Beach Park, with its sandy bathing beach, popular midway, and collection of rides, while just a few miles inland, and easily reached by one of the new "electric trolley cars," was the bustling city of Rochester.

As the years passed, automobiles became the preferred way to travel, and to accommodate them hundreds of miles of new highways were built. The impact this modernization had on cross-lake passenger boat traffic quickly became obvious. Passenger numbers dropped drastically. Then, with the more stringent safety regulations imposed by both governments following the tragic September 1949 fire that destroyed the SS *Noronic* and took the lives of 119 souls while the "Queen of the Lakes" was berthed in the Port of Toronto, the end was truly in sight. Soon the SS *Cayuga* was the lone passenger boat on Lake Ontario, but it, too, was taken out of service and eventually scrapped.

In recent years several plans have been put forward to resurrect a passenger boat service from Toronto to Queenston, with bus connections upriver to Niagara-on-the-Lake or south to Niagara Falls. A few ideas worked for a short time, but all eventually failed. Then, about a decade ago, talk turned to bringing back a Toronto-to-Rochester lake boat service, though this time the craft suggested for the route was a large catamaran operating what was described as a "fast ferry" service.

With the enthusiastic support of government officials in Rochester, a group of investors placed an order with Austral Ships of Perth, Australia, for one "Auto Express

The long-anticipated Toronto-Rochester ferry service began on June 17, 2004, when the *Spirit of Ontario 1* arrived in the pouring rain at its Toronto Terminal located just inside the Eastern Gap.

86 Class wave piercing passenger-vehicle catamaran." To be known as the *Spirit of Ontario I*, the craft was to enter service in the spring of 2004. But there were delays, and cross-lake operations didn't actually begin until June 17 of that year when the vessel arrived at Toronto's makeshift (a modern new terminal wouldn't be ready until the next year) International Ferry Terminal near the foot of Cherry Street. And while service was to be carried out year-round, financial difficulties forced the operations to be suspended on September 7, 2004. What now?

In February of the following year, the City of Rochester became the *Spirit*'s new owner, with operations turned over to Northumberland Ferries Limited, which was running a similar venture between Yarmouth, Nova Scotia, and Bar Harbor, Maine. The 2005 season began with great expectations on June 30, and though year-round trips were planned, by the end of the year finances dictated that all operations be suspended. Worse was yet to come when the City of Rochester withdrew its financial commitment and the vessel was put up for sale.

In the spring of 2007, Toronto's *Spirit of Ontario 1* was sold to FRS, a German transportation company, and was soon in operation between Tarifa, Spain, and Tangier, Morocco, under its new name *Tanger Jet II*. (Photo courtesy Gaetane Hermans)

Initially, it was believed *Spirit of Ontario I* (many still referred to the vessel as the *The Breeze*, a name chosen in a marketing campaign) would find a use operating across the English Channel. However, that didn't happen.

So just where is the *Spirit of Ontario I* today? Now owned by the transportation company FRS, it's busy ferrying passengers between Tarifa on the south coast of Spain and Tangiers, Morocco. And the craft's new name? *Tanger Jet II*. Too bad its name was changed. It would have been interesting to see the *Spirit of Ontario* skimming across the Strait of Gibraltar.

Announcing Our New Over-Night Trip

We have arranged something entirely new for the benefit of Toronto people who want a short holiday at small cost—

A Trip to Rochester and Return for $4.50

This rate is inclusive of dinner on the way over and berth coming back. You leave Toronto any afternoon at 3.30. You arrive at Charlotte (Port of Rochester) in the evening. You return through the night, reaching Toronto at 7 a.m. next morning. A delightful trip—at a very special rate.

Thousand Islands

Rochester, Montreal, Quebec and Saguenay. Leaving Toronto 3.30 p.m. daily. Special rates, including meals and berth.

Hamilton

Leaves Toronto 9 a.m., 2 p.m. and 5 p.m. Leave Hamilton 7.30 a.m., 1.30 p.m. and 5.30 p.m. Toronto time, daily, including Sunday.

Note—Hamilton City time is one hour later than Toronto time.

Niagara Camp

Steamers leave Toronto daily except Sunday, 7.30 a.m., 9 a.m., 11 a.m., 2 p.m., 3.45 p.m. and 5.15 p.m. Direct connections for Niagara Falls and Buffalo. Special time table in force on Sunday.

Grimsby Beach

Leave Toronto 8 a.m. and 9.15 p.m. Leave Grimsby 10.30 a.m. and 7.15 p.m. daily, except Sunday.

CANADA STEAMSHIP LINES, Limited

Prowling the Waters

How does that oft-heard saying go? Everything old is new again. Well, that's certainly the case when it comes to passenger boat service between Rochester, New York, and Toronto.

One of the first companies to institute such a service was the Richelieu and Ontario Navigation Co. (R. and O.) whose roots go back to 1845 when its parent, La Compagnie du Richelieu, introduced a steamboat service on the Richelieu River in Quebec. Thirty years later, following the merger of the Quebec firm with the Canadian Steam Navigation Company, a new company was formed that, under the name Richelieu and Ontario Navigation Company, began operating an integrated passenger service on Lake Ontario from Toronto to Prescott and the Thousand Islands and on to Montreal. This route, which included a stopover at the Port of Charlotte (Rochester) on the American side, became so popular that R. and O. officials were forced to add two large passenger boats to the fleet: the steam-powered sidewheelers SS *Toronto*, with a passenger capacity of 855 and built in 1899, and the SS *Kingston*, with a similar carrying capacity and built two years later. Both vessels were built at the Bertram shipyard at the west end of Toronto Harbour, a once-busy factory site that today is covered by the busy Lake Shore Boulevard–Bathurst Street intersection.

In 1913, R. and O. and several other shipping companies amalgamated under the name Canada Steamship Lines (CSL). This company continued passenger boat service throughout the Great Lakes as well as in Quebec, where the firm also plied the tourist trade in co-operation with the popular Manoir Richelieu and Hotel Tadoussac.

But CSL terminated its Great Lakes passenger business in the early 1950s. Increasingly stringent safety regulations made it economically impractical for the company to bring what had become known as the "Great White Fleet" into line. And with the end of passenger boat service on Lake Ontario, so, too, ended the Toronto-Rochester cross-lake connection.

Another popular vessel for excursions across Lake Ontario was the *Cayuga*.

It should be noted that while CSL divested itself of its passenger boats (SS *Toronto* in 1939 and SS *Kingston* in 1949), it sold SS *Cayuga* to a private organization consisting of 700 nostalgic shareholders who kept the vessel operating from Toronto to ports on the Niagara River until 1957. A few years later it, too, was scrapped.

Flights of Fancy

One of the most popular features of the annual Canadian National Exhibition is the thrilling air show that fills the sky over the waterfront on the last weekend of the fair. Now officially known as the Canadian International Air Show, the genesis of this extremely popular event goes back to 1914 when a small three-seat flying boat made daily flights over awestruck Ex crowds. Remember this was just 11 years after the Wright brothers' historic first flight at Kitty Hawk, North Carolina.

A few years later CNE officials decided to allocate one of the old Exhibition buildings to the newest wonder of the age—the flying machine. Then, in 1917, a demonstration of flying in formation was held over the fairgrounds, and again the crowds were spellbound. During the 1929 CNE, air races between Cleveland and the Exhibition waterfront were held, and a year later a triangular course was set out over Lake Ontario south of the grounds. Fair visitors would watch for hours as a flock of seaplanes battled for prize money.

In 1939 the winds of war were once more blowing in Europe, and at that year's CNE a Battle fighter-bomber, an Oxford light bomber, and a Hurricane fighter provided aerial demonstrations. By 1941 war was raging in Europe, and visitors to that year's Ex marvelled at the site of a huge (for the time) Canadian-built Bolingbrook (later renamed Blenheim) reconnaissance bomber sitting in front of the Electrical and Engineering Building (a site now occupied by the Direct Energy Centre).

The 1941 fair would be the last for five long years, and the sprawling grounds were turned into a military camp. From 1942 to 1946, fun-seeking crowds were replaced by young men and women in army, navy and air force uniforms.

When the CNE returned in the fall of 1947, there was a special appearance by several Lincoln aircraft of the Second World War's famous Dambusters Squadron, and while subsequent editions of the Ex continued to include aircraft as part of the entertainment package, their appearance could hardly be termed an air show.

In 1952 and 1953, what was billed as the National Air Show moved to the Exhibition grounds, though the event was held on the third Saturday of September, almost two full weeks after the fair closed. In 1955 the air show returned to the waterfront, but again well in advance of the CNE. However, this time the event was identified by its current name, the Canadian International Air Show. The participants included the U.S. Navy's Cougar jet fighters and the RCAF's CF-100s and T-33s.

Finally, in 1956, the timing of the show was changed to have it run coincident with the Exhibition. Incidentally, featured in that very first CNE air show were the U.S. Navy's Blue Angels aerobatic flying team and a massive American air force B-52 Stratofortress eight-engine jet bomber.

A half-century later the Canadian International Air Show continues to be one of the CNE's most popular attractions.

In 1929 the CNE's Transportation Building (which was destroyed by fire in 1974) featured a selection of aircraft, including the Curtiss "Robin," "Fledgling," and "Rambler," the last being the first Canadian-designed aircraft for the civil market. It was also acquired in small numbers by the Royal Canadian Air Force.

Airport Was Slow to Fly

January 30, 2007, saw the closing of Terminal 2 at Toronto Pearson International Airport and the opening of Terminal 1's Pier F. Both events are now part of the long and fascinating history of an airport that began life under a cloud of criticism. In fact, it was just days after officials announced in May 1937 that the location of one of Toronto's two new municipal airports would be near the small farming community of Malton that the first disparaging remarks were uttered.

Even though officials indicated that this field would only be used in the event that the main airport on the city's waterfront was closed because of inclement weather, the choice of the Malton site, located as it was miles west of the city, combined with a total lack of roads to get there and back, made the choice, as far as some were concerned, laughable. A few Royal Canadian Air Force officials even suggested that it would be useless to establish one of its air bases at the new field, since none of its members would be able to get there. To be sure, the city had looked at other possible sites for an airfield that had been a long time coming.

Other North American cities had already embraced commercial aviation and had built airfields to serve their communities. Meanwhile, Toronto officials dithered, and in doing so had thus far been left out as the flying industry continued to grow. In fact, over the years several city committees had studied the idea of building a municipal airport. However, nothing specific had ever been decided and the airport idea continued to languish.

Sure, the city was home to several small private airfields: Trethewey near Weston; others close to the Wilson Avenue and Dufferin Street intersection, including what would become known as Barker; and Leaven's Airport on Dufferin just north of Lawrence Avenue. However, none of these was suitable if the city wanted to get in on the fast-growing cross-country or international passenger service.

No doubt being embarrassed at not having the proper facilities to join the flying revolution that was sweeping the continent, the city established a committee that was instructed to come forward with workable plans and possible locations for a municipal airport.

FILEY Fact

Shortly after the city's new airport opened adjacent to the small farming community of Malton, some city councillors suggested the facility be named to honour First World War air ace Billy Bishop. However, the federal government was adamant that no Canadian airports be named after a person whatever his status. In 1984, though, the facility, which had been renamed Toronto International Airport in 1960, became Lester B. Pearson Airport. It's now Toronto Pearson International.

Now, many thought, *we're finally getting somewhere.*

Several possible locations were presented, but after studying the various alternatives it was decided that an airfield on the sandbar at the west end of the Toronto Islands was the best choice for the new airport. However, realizing that inclement weather brought on by the field's proximity to Lake Ontario might make safe flying hazardous, it was agreed that a backup airfield would be built somewhere north of the city. That *somewhere* would be close to the community of Malton.

During the time between the city's decision to build its "main" airport on the island and the island field actually becoming operational, newer passenger planes had increased in size. As a result, the "standby" airport near Malton, where expansion of runways, taxiways, and aprons was easily accomplished, soon took over as the city's primary landing field. And as the public took to flying in ever-increasing numbers, it became necessary to build larger and larger passenger facilities. A long, one-level addition with a turnstile-controlled observation deck on the roof was added to the original 1939 terminal in 1954. Exactly 10 years later, the revolutionary Aeroquay was built and won numerous awards.

On June 15, 1972, the first stage of Terminal 2 was completed, followed in 1991 by the opening of Terminal 3. A new Terminal 1 replaced the old one in 2004. The old Terminal 1 was demolished, and Terminal 2 is slated for complete demolition by the end of 2008.

The first structure to be built as a terminal building at the new Malton Airport replaced the former Chapman farmhouse and was a direct copy of the Toronto Island Airport's terminal, which still stands. Obviously, the designer of this postcard has taken some licence with the airport's arrival and departure timetable.

Malton Airport, Toronto, Canada

All Aboard the TTC

It was on February 26, 1966, that Toronto's subway system was more than doubled in length with the opening of the first phase of the new Bloor-Danforth line. Actually, and to be historically accurate, the line had welcomed its first 1,200 riders the day before, but they were invited guests who rode the two celebration trains along with Prime Minister Lester B. Pearson and Ontario Premier John Robarts, who jointly declared the new subway open.

The following day, February 26, saw the first phase of the 19-station line from Keele Street at the west end to Woodbine at the east open to the public. Interestingly, the Toronto Transit Commission had planned for a day of free rides, but when some enterprising youngsters were discovered selling the souvenir tokens for less than the regular six-for-a-dollar price, officials promptly curtailed this munificent gesture. Initially, the TTC operated a controversial "integrated" service whereby subway passengers were able to ride downtown or cross-town from any station on the Bloor-Danforth line without changing trains. However, the confusion, frequent delays, and numerous safety concerns resulted in this trial being abandoned after just six months.

The birth of the Bloor-Danforth subway, however, didn't occur without criticism from detractors. In fact, even as the Yonge subway was in the planning stages it was well understood that the city's next underground line would be built along Queen Street. However, rather than a full-fledged subway like the new Yonge line would be, the Queen route would feature regular streetcars that would descend from street level to operate through a tunnel that would be constructed from Strachan Avenue in the west to the Don River, or to Pape or even Logan in the east if the money was available.

Passengers board a westbound Bloor-Danforth streetcar at Bay, circa 1950.

This project was on the books for years until it was placed on the back burner following a decision by Metro Toronto Council in April 1959 to go ahead with two multi-million-dollar projects. The first would be a two-mile-long subway under University Avenue that would hook onto the south end of the five-year-old Yonge line, increasing the number of existing subway stations by a half-dozen. (The University line opened on February 28, 1963.)

The other scheme would be an eight-mile-long, 19-station cross-town subway that would do much to help alleviate the traffic gridlock that had slowed the existing surface streetcars to the point where the trip from Keele to Woodbine was taking nearly an hour. It was predicted the subway would cover the same distance in just over 20 minutes. Oh, and that Queen streetcar subway? It continued to be the subject of discussion for decades. Even now it's sometimes mentioned when transportation planners search for new ways to move traffic through the city's congested core.

While on the subject of streetcars, they had been in use over various parts of Bloor Street since the late 1800s. In late 1918 the newly constructed Prince Edward Viaduct over the Don Valley permitted the Bloor streetcars to connect with the fast-growing part of town described back then as "out the Danforth." The use of streetcars along this corridor increased over the years. Many long-time Torontonians will remember when streetcars—often in the form of so-called Peter Witt "trains" (a Peter Witt "motor" pulling a trailer) and later as M-Us (multiple-units consisting of a pair of coupled PCC streamliners)—would shuttle between the two legendary streetcar loops, Jane on the west and Luttrell on the east. They were usually jammed to the doors. The Jane-Luttrell (or if you were headed in the other direction, Luttrell-Jane) service was introduced in the mid-1920s and remained in its entirety until the Bloor-Danforth subway opened in 1966.

In this circa 1930 photo, a large Peter Witt train (motor and trailer) makes its way north at the busy Bloor Street intersection.

But even then the good old streetcar still had a place on Bloor and Danforth, providing shuttle service from the two initial subway terminals at Keele and Woodbine to and from the aforementioned loops. Streetcars weren't entirely banished from Bloor and Danforth until the east and west extensions of the Bloor-Danforth subway to Warden and Islington, respectively, opened in 1968. To complete the picture the extensions to Kennedy and Kipling opened in 1980.

Some of the information above was gleaned from a Toronto Transportation Society newsletter. The society is a wonderful resource for those interested in Toronto's transit history.

A Desire for Streetcars

When rapid transit first appeared on Toronto city streets, the year was 1861 and the "rapid" part of the new system was provided by horses. In fact, at one time during the city's horse-car era well over 1,000 animals were stabled in three areas of the young city just off Yonge Street in the suburban Village of Yorkville and in ramshackle old buildings in and around Front and Frederick streets downtown. The first route to be operated by the these primitive cars was from the St. Lawrence Hall on King Street at Jarvis to the Yorkville Town Hall on Yonge just north of Bloor. The maximum fare charged by the private operator of the system was five cents, with the cars to operate 16 hours per day in the summer and 14 hours per day in winter. One other regulation imposed by the city—something that made

The Streetcars for Toronto Committee meets in 1972. Believe it or not, that's me at the far left. (Photo courtesy Steve Munro)

the horses happy but made real rapid transit difficult—was the speed of these cars. That was limited to six miles per hour.

It quickly became obvious that the limitations imposed by the use of horses (feed bills, sickness, and other, more obvious considerations) meant that another form of motive power was needed. In Europe experiments using the latest wonder of the age, electricity, to propel little cars full of passengers along a miniature railway had proven successful. It wasn't long before electric motors were modified and adapted to power larger vehicles along steel rails embedded in city streets. The power feeding these motors was retrieved from overhead wires using a small cage-like apparatus that trolled along behind the vehicle. This so-called "troller" eventually gave rise to the term *trolley*, as in trolley car.

In Toronto the horse cars were phased out starting in 1892, and by the end of 1894, electrically-powered "motors" were in operation on all the city lines. However, unlike the European experimental vehicles that incorporated a "troller" to collect the power from the overhead, the Toronto cars were fitted with trolley poles. This was a world's first. The idea was perfected at the Toronto Industrial Exhibition in 1884 and was the brainchild of Belgian-born inventor Charles Van de Poel, who worked closely with Toronto pioneer electrician John J. Wright.

Electric streetcars soon became commonplace on numerous Toronto thoroughfares, and even those that didn't have them, like University Avenue, often showed up on plans that prophesied an ever-expanding city street railway system.

With the arrival of the Toronto Transportation Commission (later renamed the Toronto Transit Commission) on September 1, 1921, streetcar systems that had developed in communities outside the city proper came under the commission's management. As a result, street railway mileage grew dramatically.

Eventually, though, pressure was brought to bear on many North American electric streetcar operators, including the TTC, by the large bus and tire manufacturers and gasoline companies who offered great incentives to convert from electrically powered equipment to rubber-tired, gasoline-powered vehicles. To its credit the TTC didn't bite. But as the years passed it became apparent that with fewer and fewer suppliers of the materials and equipment necessary to keep the TTC's streetcar fleet, overhead, and tracks in good repair, the idea of abandoning the streetcar in Toronto was gaining momentum. In fact, to start the ball rolling a commission report dated September 21, 1972, recommended the replacement of streetcars on St. Clair Avenue with trolley coaches and those on Rogers Road with diesel buses. The end of the streetcar in Toronto was in sight.

And that's when a citizen-based group known as the Streetcars for Toronto Committee, and mentored by city aldermen Paul Pickett and William Kilbourn, swung into action. A few of the members on the committee that come to mind were Andrew Biemiller, Steve Munro, John Bromley, Chris Prentice, Howard Levine, and myself. There were others, but that was more than 35 years ago (yikes), and I simply forget all the names.

We prepared a substantial report outlining the merits of the streetcar (interestingly, there was no mention of streetcars not needing petroleum products as that was a non-issue back then) and submitted it. In doing so we convinced the TTC to alter its position. That decision, made at the commission meeting held on November 7, 1972, confirmed that Toronto would remain a streetcar city.

Ball-oil or Ball-iol?

"The next station is Osgoode ... Osgoode Station ... arriving at Osgoode ... Osgoode Station!"

Tens of thousands of TTC passengers hear the above and a variety of similar pre-recorded announcements every day. That voice they hear in the subway and on the Scarborough RT is that of Sue Bigioni, while the clear, emphatic tones heard in all the surface vehicles belongs to Cheryl Bomé. Both ladies are TTC employees and work at the commission's sprawling Hillcrest complex on Bathurst Street at Davenport Road. These automated announcements are a far cry from the good old days when the bus driver, conductor (on the two-man streetcars), or operator was responsible for letting people know where they were. Because the manner in which these announcements was presented was at the discretion of these fellows (some women, too, when they were called on to operate some of the vehicles during the Second World War), they occasionally became a source of humour. Take for instance the now politically incorrect statement heard on some streetcars headed downtown: "Not sure what to do tonight? Why not take your wife to Yonge and shoot her." Shuter ... get it?

On subway trains and the RT, the station names to be announced are determined by devices adjacent to the tracks and selected from a database onboard the train. Surface vehicles, on the other hand, use the global positioning system (GPS) to determine the next stop on the route. The corresponding pre-recorded announcement is selected from a database onboard the bus or streetcar.

Someday I'll have to ride the 35 Jane bus to hear how Baby Point is pronounced (it should be *Bawby* after early French settlers in the Windsor area). Then there's Roncesvalles (the proper pronunciation of this small community in Spain needs to be heard to be appreciated). And don't get me started on Spadina (*Spadeena*, a First Nation word for a hill) or Trethewey (George Trethewey had a farm nearby). And while the 97 Yonge bus no longer stops at Balliol—named for a college at Oxford, as is the nearby Merton—it was common to hear the guys on the old Yonge streetcars call it *Balloil*, pronouncing the word as if the last three letters were the stuff in a car engine.

Happy Anniversary

August 15 marks the day in 1892 when the city's first electrically powered streetcar trundled up Church Street. Citizens, who had been used to horse-drawn streetcars in their town since they were introduced in 1861, lined the street in stunned silence as they watched the new cars operate seemingly by magic. Electricity was still a relatively unknown mystery, and many riders initially refused to board the cars, warned away by the daily newspapers trumpeting that "they were the work of the devil. Don't believe us? When you board these devil cars look at your pocket watch. It will have stopped—obviously the devil is in it."

In truth the magnetic field around the unshielded electric motor had magnetized the watch's mechanism. Unfortunately, few understood the phenomenon, and for a time people would stand back and let the electric car pass, opting for the simplicity of the one pulled by a horse.

In spite of the concerns, things eventually settled down, and by August 31, 1894, all streetcar horsepower was generated by electricity.

FILEY *Fact*

Contrary to what some people may think, the Civic Holiday in August wasn't named to honour a Japanese automobile. Actually, in Toronto the holiday, first held on Thursday, September 12, 1861, is officially known as Simcoe Day. It was moved to the first Monday in August in 1899.

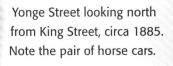

Yonge Street looking north
from King Street, circa 1885.
Note the pair of horse cars.

Tunnel Vision

It's interesting to look at how a plan put forward
by the Swansea Construction Company, the people
who built the first stretch of the Gardiner Expressway, would have drastically changed the way today's
traffic navigates past the Canadian National Exhibition fairgrounds as well as how transit riders
would get into and out of the park.

The idea was the brainchild of R.T. Lyons, Swansea's chief engineer. If implemented it would have seen the second phase of the multi-lane Gardiner Expressway
(the first phase, the stretch between the Humber and Jameson, opened on August 8,
1958) built in a large tunnel adjacent to and under the north end of the CNE grounds.

A horse-drawn streetcar operated by
the privately owned Toronto Street
Railway Company, westbound at
King and Simcoe streets, circa 1880.

SUBWAY ROOF

In this "doctored" August 8, 1958, aerial view of the northwest part of Exhibition Place, we see the layout of a combined expressway/streetcar tunnel along the north edge of the park. Note that the Gardiner Expressway doesn't appear in the photo. Interestingly, the first section of the Gardiner would open between the Humber River and Jameson Avenue the very day this photo was taken.

This tunnel would have run from Spencer Avenue (just west of the CNE) to Strachan Avenue and would have included provisions for a below-grade streetcar line with stops serving both the Coliseum and the Grandstand. When Lyons first approached Metro officials with his idea, it was immediately rejected. The second phase was to be elevated from Jameson to Spadina, and that was that! "Big Daddy" Fred Gardiner's mind was made up. Then, on the day before the first phase of the expressway was to open, it was announced that the tender call for the "elevated" second phase would be delayed until Lyons's notion could be studied further.

One major reason for examining the tunnel idea more was identified by city politician Ford Brand, who was convinced that a streetcar line through the CNE grounds would have to come "sooner or later." Interestingly, in 1996 the original CNE streetcar loop, located south of the future Coliseum, was relocated to the north side the building, with the possibility of eventually extending it farther west. Although not in a tunnel, at least part of Lyons's scheme came to pass.

Other advantages to the tunnel idea, according to its promoter, included an annual income of $1 million in parking revenue from cars parking on top of the tunnel. In addition, landfill from the tunnel excavation, worth more than $1.25 million, could be used to create a new 25-acre park along the CNE's waterfront (shades of the future Ontario Place that opened 13 years after the tunnel proposal was unveiled).

As great as the idea sounded at the time, it went no further, and the next stage in the creation of the Gardiner was an elevated structure that opened as far as Spadina Avenue at the end of June 1962.

Bridges to the Past

Today those of us who use the Don Valley Park-way on a regular basis pay little or no attention to the two old bridges that span the Don River just south of the high-level bridge that conveys Queen Street traffic over the Don. The old steel-truss bridge was erected in 1900 to carry Eastern Avenue traffic over the river. Then, during the planning of the stretch of the new Don Valley Parkway that was to connect with the Gardiner Expressway (which opened in 1964), officials decided to reroute Eastern Avenue, from the point where it formerly crossed the river, onto a new high-level structure. In doing so they also decided to abandon the old bridge. And there it sits to this day. It's truly "the bridge to nowhere."

Just to the north of it is another old bridge, this one of the covered variety.

Eastern Avenue Bridge over the Don River, circa 1952. Note the Consumers' Gas "covered bridge" to the left of the view.

The same view in 2005. The old Eastern Avenue Bridge is now the "bridge to nowhere." The gas company's bridge is still there.

Built in 1929 to carry pipes from the Consumers' Gas manufacturing facilities in and around the Front and Parliament street intersection, this unusual structure was erected to replace an earlier bridge that had collapsed into the river while being repainted. With gas and ammonia fumes escaping into the air and several painters floundering in the water, the event could have had serious consequences. Fortunately, police and Consumers' Gas workers worked quickly to rectify the situation.

Not far from where the two photos in this column were taken, a new sign has appeared, indicating that planning is underway by the city, the Ontario Realty Corporation, and the Toronto Waterfront Revitalization Corporation to create a new mixed-use community in the West Don Lands area (roughly Queen and Parliament streets to the north and west, the CN rail corridor to the south, and the Don River to the east. (Anyone remember the Ataritiri plan of the late 1980s?) The project will feature residential, commercial, and recreational components plus provisions for protection against the inevitable flooding of the Don as it has done since the beginning of time. Stay tuned.

FILEY *Fact*

Parking and speeding are two serious concerns facing today's officials and police officers in Toronto. But these problems aren't new. As far back as 1816, a regulation was put in place in the Town of York to ensure that: 1) "carts and carriages left in the streets shall be arranged along the sides in a regular manner on a penalty of five shillings," and 2) "No person shall race or run horses in the streets on the penalty of five shillings."

9

Toronto at Play

Canadian National Exhibition. Toronto.
The Finish Line before the Grand Stand.

Ex Marks the Spot

Visitors to the Canadian National Exhibition will notice there are a couple of pretty significant changes going on down there. For instance, the building that had originally been built and officially opened with great fanfare during the 1961 fair by then Prime Minister John Diefenbaker to house the Hockey Hall of Fame has almost disappeared. Nearby, the new 20,000-seat BMO soccer stadium has materialized. It serves as home field for Toronto FC, the city's newest professional sports team.

Many long-time CNE visitors will be well aware that this is by no means the first stadium (or even second, third, or fourth) to grace Exhibition Place, or Exhibition Park, as the place used to be called in more tranquil times. In fact, as recently as early 1999, the once highly popular Exhibition Stadium stood within an enthusiastic baseball throw to the southeast of the new soccer stadium.

Exhibition Stadium opened in 1948 with the title CNE Grandstand, and by the time all the alterations and additions were completed and the Toronto Blue Jays baseball team had taken up temporary residence in 1977, it could seat well in excess of the original 22,000 spectators for which it had been designed. A series of planned explosions reduced the structure to rubble one cold January day in 1999.

While Exhibition Stadium was the best known of all the CNE's grandstands, it certainly wasn't the first. That honour goes to the one that opened coincident with the inauguration of the very first Exhibition, then called the Toronto Industrial Exhibition, way back in 1879. It was replaced by a new, larger structure in 1895 which, sadly, was consumed by flames in 1906. Wind-blown embers from that mammoth conflagration also caused a fire that quickly engulfed the magnificent Crystal Palace several hundred yards away. Today's glass-domed Horticulture Building now stands on the site of the Palace.

In 1907 a new grandstand was built to replace the old one, and it, too, succumbed to flames in 1946. The fourth CNE grandstand was ready for the 1948 edition of the fair. Ironically, the first major event in that ultra-modern (for the time) structure was a soccer game featuring Manchester United.

FILEY *Fact*

Another city landmark that has given people difficulties over the years is the Princes' Gates at the CNE. This time the trouble concerns the way the structure's name is pronounced or spelled. Factually, the word in question is the plural possessive form of *prince* which, in this instance, refers to Edward, the Prince of Wales, and his brother, Prince George, the Duke of Kent. The boys attended the 1927 edition of the CNE where they dedicated what was to be called the Diamond Jubilee of Confederation Gates. Because the boys did the honours, though, the Princes' Gates became the only natural choice for the structure's moniker.

The Agony of Defeat

Back in early 1954 the International Ice Hockey Federation World Championship was scheduled to be held in Stockholm, Sweden. Canada's entry, if one could be found, was expected to play more than 40 exhibition and series games, for which there would be no financial compensation. All the money from ticket sales would stay in Europe.

In addition, as had happened in past tournaments, European hockey fans continued to be critical of the rough-and-tumble way Canadians played the game. These two factors certainly made it difficult for the Canadian Amateur Hockey Association to find a willing participant. Nevertheless, one was finally located. A Senior B amateur team from Toronto's suburban East York was selected. Known as the Lyndhursts, the feisty club went overseas and easily won the tournament's first six games.

Then the Canadians came up against Russia's Dynamo hockey team. Most people expected the club from Canada, the birthplace of hockey, to trounce the guys in the funny shirts and makeshift equipment. But that was not to be, and the Canadians went down to defeat 7–2. When news of the unexpected outcome arrived back home, there was shock and outrage. Canada defeated by the Russians? Impossible!

One person who was particularly bitter about Canada's trouncing was Connie Smythe who, in 1927, had taken the existing National Hockey League Toronto St. Patricks team, added some talent and muscle, and presented his hometown with a new club, the Toronto Maple Leafs. Between 1927 and 1954, the team—the pride of the city—won the prestigious Stanley Cup seven times.

Smythe was so incensed when he heard of Canada's defeat at the hands, sticks, and skates of the Dynamos that he offered to have his Leafs go up against the Russians, in Russia, and teach them a hockey lesson they would never forget. There was one condition, however: someone would have to raise the cash to send the Maple Leafs overseas. Smythe was proud and patriotic, but he was also frugal. And the trip would have to wait until the Stanley Cup champion for 1953–54 had been decided.

As it turned out, the Toronto team wouldn't have to wait that long since the boys in blue were eliminated in the playoff semifinals by the Detroit Red Wings who, in turn, were beaten by the Montreal Canadiens. And the money to send the Leafs to Russia? It wasn't long before several prominent citizens, including Toronto Mayor Allan Lamport and his nemesis, Metro Toronto Chairman Fred Gardiner, were out beating the bushes for the necessary $50,000.

That quest, however, ended almost before it began. In an unexpected telegram from Russian authorities, the proposed match was declared a no-go. The reason? The city of Moscow had no artificial rinks, and with the warmer-than-usual weather the Soviet city had been experiencing, all the natural ice rinks had melted. As a result, the much-anticipated grudge match had to be cancelled. So, could our guys have beaten their guys? We'll never know.

The Hockey Leafs Are Born

As Toronto hockey fans searched the sports pages of the February 18, 1927, editions of the city's newspapers looking for the score of the previous night's NHL game at the Arena on Mutual Street, they were surprised to discover that the long-familiar

hometown team's name was nowhere to be found. Most people didn't realize that the team they had known for the past seven and a half seasons as the Toronto St. Patricks had undergone a name change. The club was now called the Toronto Maple Leafs.

Many fans wondered if the name switch plus brand-new uniforms and different management would shake the team out of the doldrums. Thus far in the 1926–27 season the club had won only nine games, leaving the team tied for last place in the 10-team league.

A hockey program from the Mutual Street Arena in downtown Toronto, the site of the first Toronto Maple Leafs hockey game, which took place in 1927.

But a revival was not to be, and by the end of the season the newly renamed team had won a mere 15 games out of the 44 played, putting it last in its division and marginally ahead of two even worse teams in the league's other division. The Toronto Maple Leafs' first season was a disaster. But things would improve, and to date the team under the Leafs name has won 11 Stanley Cups (the franchise won another two Cups under previous monikers). Unfortunately, the last time was over 40 years ago—well before many of the fans who now watch the Leafs were even born. Oh well, there's always next year!

The history of professional hockey in Toronto leading up to the debut of the Leafs in 1927 is both fascinating and lengthy. It all began in 1909 with the creation of the National Hockey Association. Over the years Toronto was well represented in

Toronto at Play | 181

the league by teams such as the Tecumsehs, the Ontarios, the Shamrocks, and the Blueshirts. In fact, it was the unpopularity of the Blueshirts' owner, Eddie Livingstone, with the other team owners that eventually led to the dissolution of the NHA.

It wasn't long before a new league, this one without Livingstone to bother them, came into being in 1917. It was called the National Hockey League. But the owners of the teams in this league felt it wasn't practical to operate without a team representing the nation's largest English-speaking city. The fact that Toronto interests were in the process of installing artificial ice in the old Arena on Mutual Street in downtown Toronto may also have had something to do with the league's interest in Ontario's capital. When work was completed, the Arena would be the only artificial rink in all of eastern Canada.

So, with those concerns in mind, the NHL awarded the owners of the Arena a franchise. Naturally enough, the team was called the Toronto Arenas, and it went on to win the Stanley Cup in the new league's inaugural season.

However, for financial reasons and ongoing legal difficulties with Eddie Livingstone, the Arenas pulled out of the NHL in early 1919, returning for the 1919–20 season under a different name, one the new owners hoped would appeal to the large number of Irish living in the city. This time the team was called the Toronto St. Patricks. Then, in 1927, the legendary Connie Smythe arrived on the scene. He had learned that the St. Pats franchise was up for sale (more legal problems with the annoying Eddie Livingstone continued to pester the club) to either Montreal or Philadelphia interests. This was, as far as Connie was concerned, unthinkable. Contacting as many of his business acquaintances as he could, he was able to raise the $160,000 the St. Pats owners wanted for the franchise. When the deal was done, it was decided to change the team's name once more, this time to the Maple Leafs, perhaps after the badge Smythe had worn on his uniform overseas during the Great War, or perhaps after the leaf symbol that had adorned the team jerseys of Canada's gold medal–winning hockey team during the first Winter Olympics, held at Chamonix, France, three years earlier.

Interestingly, when rumours started circulating that there were changes coming for the St. Pats, some of the city's newspapers suggested that one of those changes would see the team dressed in either green and white or possibly red and white. But when the team's players took to the ice on February 17, 1927, they did so in white and blue uniforms. For the very first time the name Toronto Maple Leafs was emblazoned on their chests.

CHILDREN LEARN TO SWIM

Supervised Swimming Stations are maintained by the City at **SUNNYSIDE, WESTERN SAND BAR, FISHERMAN'S ISLAND,** and on the **DON,** above Winchester Street.

Street Cars are provided daily by the Toronto Railway Company to carry children to these stations.

ALL FREE OF CHARGE

TIME-TABLE OF FREE STREET CARS

To Sunnyside Swimming Station

Cars leave **KEELE AND DUNDAS STS. AT 1.00 P.M.**, via Dundas and Roncesvalles. Returning, leave Sunnyside at 4 p.m.

Cars leave **ROYCE AND LANSDOWNE AVES. AT 1.00 P.M.**, via Lansdowne, Dundas and Queen. Returning, leave Sunnyside at 4 p.m.

Cars leave **VAN HORNE AND DOVERCOURT AT 1.00 P.M.**, via Dovercourt Road and Queen. Returning, leave Sunnyside at 4 p.m.

To Don Swimming Station

Cars leave **C.P.R. AND YONGE ST. AT 1.00 P.M.**, via Yonge, Carlton, Gerrard and Broadview to Danforth. Returning, leave Danforth at 4 p.m.

Cars leave **GERRARD AND GREENWOOD AT 1.30 P.M.**, via Gerrard and Broadview to Danforth. Returning, leave Danforth at 4.15 p.m.

To Fisherman's Island Station

Cars leave **KINGSTON RD. AND QUEEN AT 1.30 P.M.**, via Queen, King, Church and Front to Yonge St. Returning, leave Yonge and Front at 4.05 p.m.

To Western Sandbar Station

Cars leave **CHRISTIE AND DUPONT AT 1 P.M. AND 2.30 P.M.**, via Dupont and Bathurst to Front St. Returning, leave Front and Bathurst at 3 p.m. and 4.45 p.m.

BOATS CONNECT WITH CAR SERVICES

THE TORONTO RAILWAY CO.

A 1916 newspaper ad outlining details of the new "Free Bathing Car."

Streetcar to Swim Classes

In the past there have been far too many stories concerning accidental drowning involving both adults and children. The whole idea of water safety has always been of great concern in Toronto. In fact, following a spate of accidental drowning involving youngsters in the spring of 1910, the privately operated Toronto Street Railway Company made an interesting offer to the city. In a letter to Mayor Reginald Geary, R.J. Fleming, the company president, wrote:

We believe it would be a fine thing for the community if every boy and girl would learn to swim. For the purpose of encouraging them to do so my company is prepared to place at the disposal of the boys and girls of our city on every afternoon (except Sundays) during the remainder of the summer holidays and free of charge all the special cars on different lines that will be necessary to transport them to and from the respective free swimming stations throughout the city. We make this offer on the condition that the City Council provide at these various swimming stations a sufficient number of instructors and assistants for the purpose of properly caring for the children's lives and furthering the object in view.

The city balked at the idea of providing anything more than supervised facilities for the children. In fact, as R.C. Harris, the property commissioner, stated in his return letter, it was utterly impractical to provide swimming instruction at all the stations operated by the city. He went on: "It is hard enough to teach boys in a pool, but out on a beach it is a matter of the utmost difficulty."

Nevertheless, the streetcar company went ahead with its offer, and soon what became known as "Free

Bathing Cars" were roaming downtown streets carrying hundreds of the city's little ones to and from supervised bathing stations at Sunnyside, on the Don River (at the old Winchester Street Bridge), at Fisherman's Island (near the foot of today's Cherry Street), and at a place over on the Toronto Islands known as the Western Sandbar (the site of today's Hanlan's Point).

With the creation of the new municipally controlled Toronto Transportation Commission in 1921, this unique service, now paid for by the city, continued with as many as 20 cars during the Great Depression. After the outbreak of the Second World War and restricted holiday traffic with the rationing of tires and gasoline, the "Free Bathing Cars" gained in popularity once more. However, as soon as hostilities ended and people began to leave the city during the summer months, the number of children using the cars dropped drastically. On August 9, 1950, one lonely streetcar with only eight children onboard made its way to Sunnyside Beach. After that vehicle's return to the car house, the era of the "Free Bathing Car" came to an end.

One of the most popular "bathing stations" was this one at Sunnyside, seen here in 1931.

10

Toronto Streetscapes

Locked on the Grid

When you look at a modern map of Toronto, it soon becomes apparent that the vast majority of the city's 10,033 streets, roads, avenues, and lanes run either east-west or north-south. That rather mundane grid pattern, disregarding as it does the use of any of the natural ravines, valleys, or watercourses as possible routings for thoroughfares, actually came about as a result of a survey of the area prepared in the summer of 1793 by Alexander Aitkin, the deputy surveyor general, on orders from Lieutenant Governor John Graves Simcoe.

This was the second plan prepared by Aitkin, the first having been done six years earlier on orders from Lord Dorchester, Simcoe's superior. Nothing ever came of that plan, which had a typical English-style townsite located between today's Spadina Avenue and Toronto Street, stretching north to about Gerrard Street.

Simcoe's subsequent plan for the town, which he named York after Frederick, the Duke of York, King George III's second eldest son, was laid out by Aitkin closer to where the meandering Don River flowed into Toronto Bay. It was at this end of the harbour that Simcoe established the shipyards where vessels were built to protect his new town from what he perceived as an impending invasion from south of the border.

Aitkin's townsite consisted of 10 blocks in a typical military grid and was enclosed by today's north-south streets, George and Parliament, and the east-west thoroughfares, Adelaide and Front. These directions—north, south, east, and west—continued to be followed as York, and after 1834, Toronto grew and additional streets were added.

While there are very few exceptions to the Toronto street grid, there is one that's an obvious deviation—Davenport Road. Many thousands of years ago the northern shoreline of the prehistoric Lake Iroquois that covered today's downtown Toronto was located north of Bloor Street. Steep hills on the city's main north-south traffic arteries still reveal the ancient shoreline's presence.

FILEY Fact

Toronto, Ontario, isn't the only community with that name. There's a Toronto in Ohio, Kansas, and South Dakota. One of the largest Torontos is in the Shire of Lake Macquarie, New South Wales, Australia. No longer found on any map is the Toronto that for a short time was located in Florida. This one was the dream of railway entrepreneur and former Torontonian Henry Sweetapple. This railway crossing never grew as predicted and was eventually superseded by another junction that had the rather unusual name of Kissimmee.

It was along this twisting shoreline that First Nations people forged a trail that connected what we now call the Don and Humber rivers. Over time this passageway evolved into today's Davenport Road.

In terms of the history of this ancient route, its title is relatively new, having been named for a small house that was built in the late 1700s on the hill just to the northeast of where the route crossed today's Bathurst Street. Called Davenport, it was the first residence to be erected on the hill. Others, such as Spadina House, Russell Hill, Wychwood, Rathnelly, Oaklands, and Casa Loma, followed.

But just where the term *Davenport* came from in the first place remains unclear. Was it a variation of Devonport, an important naval facility of the time near Plymouth, England, or does it derive from the name of an officer called Davenport who was stationed at the military garrison (today's Fort York)? No one is sure. It remains a Toronto mystery.

Aching with Memories

Any trip I take these days that puts me near the intersection of Gerrard Street East and Broadview Avenue always brings back a flood of unpleasant memories. Why? Because when I was a kid and had a tooth or two to be filled—remember, there was no decay-preventing fluoride in the water back then—my mother would take me to Dr. Leggett, the Filey family dentist. I don't even know if he had a first name or how my mom found him. All I remember is that his office was above the stores at the southwest corner of the intersection. In fact, I can even recall seeing his name still imprinted in gold letters on the second-floor windows facing Gerrard Street whenever I hosted a streetcar tour that went by that corner.

The real reason my visits to Dr. Leggett were so fraught with fear was because the good doctor used gas when doing any drilling and filling. For some reason freezing wasn't his thing. To this day I remember my mother leading me back home on the streetcar while I was still in a semi-stupor after undergoing some sort of dental work.

Actually, there's an upside to my story. Once the corrective work was completed, I would get my name on the Dental Honour Roll hanging near the blackboard in Mrs. Thompson's or Mr. Garten's or Mr. Todd's room at John Fisher Public School. By the way, none of my teachers had a first name, either.

Just to the north of the dentist's office was—and still is—the Riverdale branch of the Toronto Public Library. It opened in the fall of 1910 and was one of four

This postcard view, taken circa 1911, looks west along Gerrard Street across Broadview Avenue. Note that the Toronto Public Library's Riverdale Branch still occupies the northwest corner.

A similar view in 2007.

libraries in Toronto established with funds provided by the Andrew Carnegie Foundation. The arrangement with the city was conditional on Toronto donating the land on which the libraries would be built. In exchange the foundation granted $350,000 for a new Central Library at College and St. George streets, along with the Yorkville Avenue branch, the Riverdale Branch, and a branch at Queen Street West and Lisgar Street.

Later, additional foundation money helped with the construction of the Wychwood branch on Bathurst Street, south of St. Clair Avenue West; the Beaches branch on Queen Street East; the High Park branch on Roncesvalles Avenue; the Victoria College Library; and libraries in suburban West Toronto and Mimico.

By the way, an interesting feature of the two views of the Gerrard-Broadview intersection presented here is that a streetcar appears in each. In the postcard the wooden car of the privately owned Toronto Railway Company is on the Parliament

route that ran from Gerrard and Greenwood Avenue to downtown and returned
using tracks on Gerrard, Parliament, and
Queen streets. The modern CLRV vehicle
in the more recent photo operates on the
506 Carlton and 504 King routes.

From Foe to Street Sign

Readers of my columns will be aware of my
interest in the origins of street names. And
while I usually place emphasis on the names
of thoroughfares found in the City of Toronto,
other communities also have streets with fas-
cinating origins. Toronto's neighbour to the east, the Town of Ajax, is a case in point.
Even the community's name was selected in an interesting manner. The site selected
for what would eventually evolve into the bustling Town of Ajax began as nothing
more than a collection of sprawling munitions factories located in the wide-open
countryside in what was still known as the Township of Pickering. It was in these
rudimentary buildings that nearly 40 million shells for use overseas were assembled
during the Second World War. The 3,000-acre location was selected because of its
remoteness, so that if anything went wrong, the resulting explosion would be well
away from highly populated areas.

For the first few months of its existence, the place remained nameless save for
a nearby railway siding that was identified with a wooden sign upon which was an
abbreviated and slightly modified form of the munitions company name—Defence
Industries Limited. As a result, the place soon became known as DILCO.

Since the factory was located miles from the nearest established town, the government undertook the job of building housing facilities to serve the needs of some
of the thousands who worked at DILCO during the war years. Before long a small
number of stores were added to what was fast becoming a bustling community—
without a real name—in the middle of nowhere.

With the scuttling of the German pocket battleship *Admiral Graf Spee* off the coast
of Montevideo, Uruguay, a few months earlier still fresh in the minds of most of the
war workers, a proposal was put forward to name the community in honour of HMS

FILEY Fact

One of the suggestions we hear these days on ways to raise money to build
highways is to have those who use them pay a toll. In fact, toll charges are
nothing new. Back in the mid-1800s, getting to and from Toronto required
paying a fee at various toll houses constructed along streets such as Yonge
and Dundas and Lake Shore Road. The money collected was used to keep
those roads passable. Tolls were abolished on December 31, 1896, following the city's agreement to eliminate fees charged to out-of-town farmers
for the use of space at the St. Lawrence Market.

Ajax, the flagship of the Royal Navy's flotilla of Allied warships that had forced the German warship to seek refuge in the South American port. (The other two ships in the flotilla were HMS *Achilles* and HMS *Exeter*.)

On December 19, *Admiral Graf Spee*, minus its crew and most of its officers who had been left ashore, sailed from Montevideo. Then, on orders from the vessel's captain, Hans Langsdorff, the battleship was scuttled in the estuary waters off the River Plate. The following day the captain and his crew evacuated to Buenos Aires. It was there that Langsdorff, having retired to his hotel room, spread the ship's battle ensign across the bed, lay down on it, and shot himself.

The loss of the *Admiral Graf Spee* was one of the few high points for the Allies in a war that had thus far been dominated by German victories.

The suggestion to name the community after the British warship received unanimous acceptance. Ajax it would be. Interestingly, the town officials went even farther—the town's main street honours the flotilla commander Henry Harwood, while many of the other thoroughfares in town were named in honour of several of the officers and crew members of all three Allied ships.

At a recent naming of an Ajax street, things were done a lot differently. Instead of honouring a member of the Allied vessels' crew, it was decided that Captain Langsdorff would be commemorated. For obvious reasons much thought went into the decision to select this particular name for one of the town's residential streets. It was felt that the actions of Langsdorff in scuttling his ship instead of engaging the Royal Navy vessels awaiting him, as had been ordered by the German High Command, had saved countless lives of crew members not only on his ship but on the Allied vessels awaiting *Admiral Graf Spee*'s run for the high seas. Present to dedicate the street officially was Mrs. Inge Nedden, Langsdorff's daughter, who, along with her husband, was visiting Ontario.

Town of Ajax Mayor Steven Parish (left), Mrs. Inge Nedden, Captain Langsdorff's daughter, and her husband, Dr. Ruediger Nedden, at the special street-naming ceremony held on October 6, 2007.

Our Streets Are Paved in History

Many of the streets in the old part of Toronto reflect the close ties the community had with English royalty, so we have King Street (for King George III) and George and Frederick streets (for his two eldest sons). There's another downtown Toronto thoroughfare with an obvious royal connection and that, of course, is Queen Street. But the choice of that name had nothing to do with King George III. Queen was named some years later in honour of Victoria, who ascended to the throne in June 1837.

City officials wanted to recognize their new monarch, but since all the streets in the three-year-old city had already been christened, to do so would require changing the name of an existing thoroughfare. This they did by turning Lot Street, a name selected years earlier because of the 100-acre property lots that originally fronted on it, into the much more patriotic Queen Street.

As Toronto grew in both population and area, new streets were names, and choices that would once again reflect the community's loyalty to the Crown, would be to use the surnames of the various Canadian governors general who had been appointed over the years. And thus today we have Lisgar, Argyll, Dufferin, Stanley, Connaught, Devonshire, Willingdon, Bessborough, and Tweedsmuir.

Oh, and don't forget Lansdowne Avenue. This thoroughfare was named in honour of Sir Henry Charles Keith Petty-Fitzmaurice, the fifth Marquess of Lansdowne. No doubt his title was chosen because no signboard was long enough to take the whole name. Lansdowne had attended Eton and Oxford and had been an MP in the government of William Gladstone before being appointed Canada's fifth governor general. He served from 1883 to 1888 after which he returned to England and continued to serve the British government for another dozen or so years.

The Marquess of Lansdowne, who served as Canada's fifth governor general, had one of the city's main thoroughfares named in his honour. The name of the street was nearly usurped by that of Sir Arthur Currie, a Canadian hero of the Great War.

Unfortunately, Lansdowne's heretofore unsullied name was tarnished in the fall of 1917 when, at a time the Great War wasn't going too well for the Allies, he suggested that England sue for peace with Germany. When the local newspapers ran this story, many Torontonians who had sons serving overseas or had lost loved ones in battles such as the recent victory at Vimy Ridge took exception to Lansdowne's unpatriotic comments.

Tempers flared, especially among those living in the extremely pro-British Earlscourt area of the city. Soon there were calls to change Lansdowne Avenue's name to something more loyal and jingoistic. To this end, many citizens suggested Currie to honour Sir Arthur Currie, who had recently been appointed commander of the Canadian Corps.

Born in Strathroy, Ontario, Currie often voiced his opinion that Canadian members of the military should be under the command of Canadian officers. This suggestion wasn't well received by the British generals. Nevertheless, many believe that Currie was largely responsible for the Canadian victory at Vimy Ridge. In fact, British wartime Prime Minister David Lloyd George went so far as to suggest that had the war continued past November 11, 1918, he might have appointed Currie commander of *all* British forces.

As for the change of the Toronto street name, we know nothing more happened and the street remains Lansdowne. However, had things been different in 1918 we would be getting off the streetcar now at Queen and Currie.

Streets Paved the Way

When the subject of Toronto's historic thoroughfares comes up, it's usually Yonge and Dundas streets that get the most attention. While both were concepts put forward by Upper Canada's first lieutenant governor, John Graves Simcoe, each was to serve a different purpose. The former, Yonge Street, was named in honour of Sir George Yonge, an old friend and political ally of Simcoe.

Yonge Street was originally intended to be the quickest way to get reinforcements from established British forts along the upper lakes to the young provincial capital of York in the event of invasion of the British colonies by American forces. The possibility of invasion was to remain a major concern as long as the U.S. government believed it should control all of North America.

Cronyism has always existed in Toronto: Sir George Yonge (1731–1812).

Dundas Street, on the other hand, was initially devised by Simcoe as a commercial trading route between York and Dundas, Upper Canada, a community named in honour of Sir Henry Dundas, secretary of state for the colonies. Although now a suburb of Hamilton, back then Dundas was a thriving town in its own right.

Simcoe envisioned his "Dundas Highway" eventually being extended to the site of today's City of London where on the banks of the Thames River (both names show Simcoe's admiration for England) a permanent provincial capital would be established. He reasoned that the "temporary" site at York was much too close to the enemy to be a definitive choice. However, for a variety of reasons, mostly political, Simcoe's aspirations were never realized.

As ancient as both Yonge and Dundas may be, there is one thoroughfare that can be considered even older.

While the present Lakeshore Road west of the Humber River really came into its own with the influx of settlers in the 1800s, it has been suggested that the origins of this thoroughfare can be traced back to the 1750s. It was in that decade that a narrow dirt path was laid out to connect the original French fur-trading fort, Fort Toronto, on the east bank of the Humber River with its successor, Fort Rouillé, which was located just west of the Bandshell on the grounds of Exhibition Place. The eastern terminus of today's Lakeshore Road is at the bridge over the Humber River. It is a continuation of Lake Shore Boulevard, which was established in the early 1920s as part of a massive waterfront improvement program undertaken by the Toronto Harbour Commission.

Long before that, however, stagecoaches had been using the unimproved Lakeshore Road as they made their way between York (Toronto) and Niagara (Niagara-on-the-Lake). As communities such as Mimico, New Toronto, Long Branch, Port Credit, Clarkson, Oakville, Bronte, and Burlington came into being along the way, it soon became necessary to upgrade the road. In 1917 Lakeshore Road was paved and became known province-wide as the Toronto-Hamilton Highway.

An integral part of transportation along Lakeshore Road arrived in the 1890s with the establishment of the Toronto and Mimico Electric Railway and Light Company. During the following years, the company extended a rudimentary streetcar service out along Lakeshore Road, eventually reaching the Long Branch community on July 1, 1895, and the Credit River a little more than a year later. There were plans to extend the line all the way to Hamilton, but financial difficulties and the increasing use of the automobile soon put an end to that idea.

In 1920 Toronto purchased this and other privately owned electric radial lines operating outside the city and turned their operation over to Ontario Hydro. Eventually, these lines became part of the recently organized Toronto Transportation Commission. The commission's streetcar route along Lakeshore Road was soon double-tracked all the way west to the site of the present Long Branch loop, while the roadway itself was widened considerably.

On December 8, 1928, the TTC's new Lakeshore streetcar route came into being, operating initially from Brown's Line (Long Branch) to Queen Street and Roncesvalles Avenue. The route was extended a few years later all the way downtown to loop on Mutual Street just north of Queen Street. It wasn't until the summer of 1937 that the long-familiar Lakeshore route name finally disappeared when it and the Beach route (originally operating from the Humber River to Neville Park, out Queen Street East way) were combined to form part of a realigned Queen streetcar route. Today that route, with some modifications, operates as the 501 Queen line, one of the longest streetcar routes on the continent.

Stroll the Avenue

In 1894, the year that English-born sculptor Hamilton P. MacCarthy's statue of Sir John A. Macdonald was unveiled, the "view" that Canada's first prime minister had was much different than the one he has today. Back then University Avenue was lined with large mature trees, while on nearby Queen's Park Circle there were a substantial number of residences owned by the era's rich and famous. While not occupied as residences today, many of those large houses still stand, most of them now serving the various needs of the University of Toronto.

University Avenue itself has an interesting history. The thoroughfare was originally laid out as a means of access from Queen Street to the new King's College, the forerunner of the University of Toronto, which was located where the Parliament Buildings stand today. At that time University Avenue was called, naturally enough, College Avenue, or simply "The Avenue." Entrance to the college-owned thoroughfare, which in reality was just a dirt pathway, was controlled by a gateman whose dwelling sat about where the South African War Memorial is today.

King's College occupied its location at the top of "The Avenue" only briefly before school officials decided to relocate a short distance to the west. It was on this new site that the city's pioneer institute of higher learning flourished as the University of Toronto.

For a time, the King's College building served as a lunatic asylum before its eventual demolition. By 1886 work was well underway on a magnificent new structure that would occupy the site, one that would house the members, officials, and staff of the Legislative Assembly of Ontario who were stuck in a shabby collection of old buildings on Front Street, about where the CBC Building is today. Everybody, including Richard Waite, the English-born architect of the new structure (who was initially asked to simply judge the plans submitted but somehow wound up winning the competition), was ecstatic with the new buildings when they were officially opened on April 4, 1893.

Looking south down University Avenue from the lawn in front of the Legislative Buildings of Ontario, aka the Parliament Buildings, circa 1902. Note that Sir John A. Macdonald is looking at all the trees.

A similar view in 2005. Sir John is now looking *for* all the trees.

As we can see, the reason today's Parliament Buildings occupy such a picturesque site at the top of University Avenue was more a stroke of good luck than good planning.

To continue with the story of University Avenue, the fact that it's the city's widest thoroughfare came about in a rather unusual way. Today's University Avenue is actually composed of two separate streets. On the west (southbound lanes) was the former College Avenue, which as mentioned was privately owned by the university. To the east (northbound lanes) was a narrow public thoroughfare called Park Lane. Early in the twentieth century these two streets were joined to become one, and over the ensuing years skilful landscaping and frequent realignment of the two streets resulted in University Avenue's present configuration.

Looking west along Bloor Street from Avenue Road in 1922. Works crews of the newly created TTC are seen busily repairing worn-out streetcar tracks between Avenue Road and Spadina. A portion of McMaster Hall (now the Royal Conservatory of Music) can be seen to the left of the view. And look at all the trees!

The Road to Riches

Today Bloor Street, between Yonge on the east and Avenue Road on the west, is regarded by many as Toronto's version of New York City's Fifth Avenue. Lined with some of the best-known and classy stores on the continent, the thoroughfare has come a long way from the time it was simply a narrow dirt concession road laid out by surveyors through the forest that surrounded the young city to the south. In fact, the yet-to-be-named street (The Second Concession was title enough) was so remote that a six-acre plot of land at the northwest corner of the concession road where it intersected with today's Yonge Street was selected in 1826 as the site of the community's first non-sectarian cemetery. The property, which stretched along the north side of what would become today's Bloor Street to approximately where Avenue Road cuts through today, was purchased for £75 (less than $400). That little cemetery was to become the final resting place for nearly 6,000 souls by the time it closed in 1855.

Bloor was certainly not the first name given to the Second Concession Road. In fact, in the early days it had several titles, including St. Paul's Road, which it took after the building of the first church of that name in 1841; Sydenham Road, after Lord Sydenham, who was appointed governor off the Province of Canada in 1839; and eventually Toll Gate Road because of a toll gate that stood for a time just north of the Yonge corner.

But the name that stuck was that of Joseph Bloor, an early settler in the area. Born in Staffordshire, England, in 1789, Bloor arrived in the Town of York in 1819 and established a small hotel near the St. Lawrence Market. Some years later he moved north of what in 1834 had become the City of Toronto and opened a brewery in the ravine northeast of the modern Canadian Tire store on Yonge Street, not far from the Church-Davenport intersection.

Bloor became a wealthy man, and with his contemporary William Botsford Jarvis he developed numerous properties in what eventually evolved into the trendy Yorkville part of Toronto. Bloor built a large residence on the south side of the street, and it was this fact that resulted in the street having its present name.

Now, as for the other street in the photos, Avenue Road, years ago I was told the origin of this unusual name by the late Tommy Thompson, the former Metro Toronto parks commissioner. It seems sometime in the late 1800s a group of English land developers were searching the area in and around today's St. Clair-Bathurst intersection for property in which to invest. After a long and exhausting day, they decided to head back downtown. But to do so they had to

A similar view in November 2006. The Royal Ontario Museum and its unusual "Crystal" addition are under construction to the left of the view. The Park Hyatt Hotel is to the right, and there's not a tree in sight.

FILEY *Fact*

When the thoroughfare that became Avenue Road first appeared on surveyors' maps in the mid-1880s, it was more or less a continuation of College Avenue, a street we now know as University Avenue. The "College" part of the old name came from the fact that it was originally a private bridle path running north from Queen Street to the college, King's College, to be specific, a building that stood where the Parliament Buildings were to rise in the early 1890s. Years later King's College relocated farther west and was renamed the University of Toronto. Over time "The College Avenue" became simply "The Avenue." As a result, when today's Avenue Road was laid out in the mid-1880s, it was seen as the "road to The Avenue" or, as it would turn out, Avenue Road.

travel more than a mile east along the dusty Third Concession (today's St. Clair Avenue) before turning south on Yonge Street.

"There must be an easier way to get back to town," one of the group was heard to say. But there wasn't, a fact that some say resulted in one of the weary travellers suggesting, "They ought to 'ave a new road here."

Top Drawer Streets

The two views of Jarvis Street accompanying this column look north from the Shuter Street corner and are separated by the passage of approximately 80 years. They vividly exemplify the remarkable changes that have taken place in the look of most of Toronto's major streets in relatively short periods of time. Jarvis Street actually began as a simple dirt driveway leading from Queen Street north to the residence of Samuel Peters Jarvis, a two-storey brick structure built in 1824 that Jarvis dubbed Hazelburn. Twenty-three years later Jarvis tore the place down, extended the old driveway north to Bloor Street, and sold parcels of land adjacent to the new thoroughfare on which some of the city's elite built substantial dwellings. The new residents were only too proud to tell the world they lived on a stately avenue that many of them pronounced *Jawvis* Street, and not without a little smugness.

Jarvis Street looking north from Shuter Street, circa 1925.

It wasn't long before the various city guides began recommending that visitors to the city take a tally-ho coach ride along Jarvis, Church, and Sherbourne streets, some of the finest thoroughfares anywhere in the young country.

The same view in 2005. The new Grand Hotel (in the former RCMP Toronto headquarters building) is on the extreme right.

In his book *Toronto, Past and Present*, published in 1884, author C. Pelham Mulvany describes this trio of streets in these words:

> *Of all the avenues extending south from Bloor Street to Toronto Bay the noblest are Church, Jarvis and Sherbourne. Church is somewhat less aristocratic (than the others) but has all the advantage of magnificent church buildings in its course. Jarvis and Sherbourne are lined on either side through most of their extent by mansions of the upper ten. Of a summer it is pleasant to saunter down one of these streets while the thick verdure of chestnut trees is fresh with the life of June and the pink and white bunches of blossom are as beautiful as any of the exotic flowers in the lawns and gardens of the houses.*

Many of my readers will recall a time, not that long ago, when Jarvis Street was known far and wide for something other than its trees and flowers.

11

Toronto Neighbourhoods

A Neighbourhood Tale

As we all know, the condominium market in the Greater Toronto Area is hot, hot, hot. In fact, it's been estimated that more than 250 condo buildings are either in the planning stages or actually under construction throughout the city. One of the areas undergoing major changes as rows and rows of single-family dwellings are replaced by soaring condominium towers is the neighbourhood where I grew up. Whenever I go back to the streets in and around Yonge Street and Eglinton Avenue, more houses and small apartments are on the way down and more condo towers are on the way up.

Even as I write this column, the "ancient" structure that housed my old high school, North Toronto Collegiate, is destined for demolition. On the site there will be a new Tridel development that will feature a couple of condo towers to be known as the Republic of Yonge and Eglinton, and a brand-new and "eco-friendly" North Toronto Collegiate. And from what I remember from my days there (actually six years because I liked the place so much), the replacement for the aged school will come not a moment too soon.

Interestingly, the name of the school reveals just how old the collegiate and its main building are. That's because the school actually takes its name from the community in which it was built in 1912. Back then North Toronto was still a town, separate and distinct from the big city to the south. The town had been created out of the amalgamation in 1889 of the communities known as Davisville, Eglinton, and Bedford Park into what was initially the Village of North Toronto, a status that was raised to that of a town on April 7, 1890.

As the population of the Town of North Toronto grew, the number of students seeking higher education (after attending the local John Fisher and Eglinton public schools) had become too great to be accommodated in a couple of rooms on an upper floor of the old Town Hall at the northwest corner of Yonge and Montgomery. So it was that the town council decided to erect a new high school to serve the needs of the town's young people. The man who championed the construction of the high school and served as its first principal was George H. Reed.

Reed had graduated from the University of Toronto with a degree in classics and went on to teach in various schools around the province. It was while he was teaching in the high school in Markham, Ontario, that Reed was offered the position of principal of the Town of North Toronto's newly organized high school. Reed served in that capacity at both the old and new buildings until 1927 when he retired and was succeeded by Colonel F.H. Wood, another long-time school principal. George Reed died in 1931 and is buried in Mount Pleasant Cemetery.

Interestingly, the Town of North Toronto disappeared the same year the school was built, becoming a "ward" (actually Ward 9) of the City of Toronto on December 15, 1912.

It's Déjà Vu for St. Clair

As more and more people moved to Toronto in the late 1800s, it was only natural that many would forgo the congested downtown areas, favouring instead the wide-open countryside north of the city where they could find cool breezes, lower humidity and, most important, cheap land. Here the money that had been spent on rent could be used to build a house, not a big house to be sure, but something one could call his or her own.

One area that began to see a marked increase in population was along the dirt concession road that would eventually take the name St. Clair. There is some speculation, though no conclusive proof exists, that this thoroughfare took its name from Augustine St. Clare, a well-intentioned but ill-fated member of the cast in Harriet Beecher Stowe's *Uncle Tom's Cabin*. This novel has been described as the most popular book of the nineteenth century. Rumour has it that children in the Grainger family, early settlers in the Yonge–St. Clair neighbourhood, selected Augustine's surname for their pickup baseball team, painting the name and spelling it incorrectly in the process ... Clair instead of Clare ... on a board that was subsequently tacked to a nearby wooden pole, suggesting to some travellers through the area that it was, in fact, the name of the street. True or not, it makes an interesting story.

With the influx of new settlers along St. Clair, it wasn't long before communities with names like Earlscourt, Oakwood, Bracondale, and Wychwood started to take shape on what had been rolling farmland. Soon streets were laid out, houses were built, and schools were opened.

Because of the increasing population along St. Clair, many people tried to convince the privately owned Toronto Railway Company to provide streetcar service to these new communities. However, the owners of the company weren't convinced any expenditure on their part would increase profits. That, plus the fact it wasn't likely the company's franchise would be extended past 1921, resulted in nothing being done.

St. Clair Avenue looking west from near Bathurst Street, showing the land-fill over the Nordheimer ravine. In 1912 a severe storm caused the material to wash away, resulting in a major disruption to the construction of the St. Clair streetcar line.

Eventually, the city decided to build and operate its own streetcar system. To be operated under the title Toronto Civic Railways, a total of five lines were to be built, one of which would be along St. Clair. Work on this line began in 1911, but it wasn't an easy project. The undulating nature of St. Clair Avenue necessitated filling and levelling those areas where deep valleys crossed the street such as those at Ossington Avenue, Winona Drive, and Lauder Avenue. The biggest problem, however, was east of Bathurst Street where the Nordheimer Ravine crossed the right-of-way (where the mammoth Loblaw's store is today). This part of the project was time-consuming and became even more so when the initial land-fill was washed away during a storm, a complication that resulted in a major set-back. The new line was finally completed and opened in the late summer of 1913, almost two years after work began.

Another modern-day characteristic of St. Clair, its width, was also agreed upon coincident with the building of the new streetcar line. Originally just a narrow dirt trail, the city decided to take advantage of the remoteness of the street and lay out the thoroughfare wider than downtown streets. That is, instead of the standard 66-foot width, the section of St. Clair from Yonge to Avenue Road, where some substantial buildings had already been built, was laid

A similar view in the fall of 2006.

out 86 feet wide, while the long stretch from Avenue Road west to the terminus at Station Street (next to the old Grand Trunk Railway station west of today's Caledonia Road) would be 100 feet wide. It was also decided to incorporate a 33-foot-wide gravel-ballasted centre boulevard over which the streetcars would operate.

Then, in 1921 and much to the delight of a frustrated public, the municipally operated Toronto Transportation Commission took over all public transit service in the city and the St. Clair line became one of the new commission's responsibilities. Interestingly, eight years later officials decided to remove that streetcar right-of-way. Now, in a kind of déjà vu, the TTC is putting the reservation back as one feature of the revitalization of the 512 St. Clair streetcar route.

Yonge at Heart

One of the many small communities that developed on the northern outskirts of Toronto was called Newtonbook. It stretched on either side of Yonge Street between Finch's Corners (so named for John Finch, who operated a popular hotel at the southeast

Steeles Avenue, circa 1935. Just down the street is the community of Newtonbrook. Today's modern Centerpoint Mall, which initially opened in 1966 as Towne and Countrye Square, now sits astride what had for years been farmland.

corner of Yonge and Finch Avenue) and Steele's Corners (so called in tribute to Thomas Steele, who operated another popular hostelry, the Green Bush Inn, at the northwest corner of Steeles Avenue and Yonge).

As for the name Newtonbrook, it came from one of the neighbourhood houses of worship, a place that was originally called Newton's Brook Wesleyan Church. It in turn was named for a small watercourse that flowed under Yonge Street, one that pioneer settlers had called Newton's Brook in honour of the Reverend Robert Newton, one of their church's first preachers.

An important feature of the Newtonbrook community was the freight and passenger service to and from the big city to the south, provided by the big electric streetcars that rumbled up and down the "main drag." These cars were more often than not referred to as "radials," a title derived from the fact that the Yonge Street service (as well as several other lines such as those to Guelph and Woodbridge) radiated out from Toronto to serve communities surrounding the city. The first of these cars reached Newtonbrook in 1896 as part of the extension of the Yonge Street route from York Mills north to Richmond Hill. The line ultimately served Aurora, Newmarket, and smaller communities along the south shore of Lake Simcoe. In fact, today's Metro Road utilizes the radial cars' abandoned right-of-way.

One year after the Toronto Transportation Commission assumed operation of all the privately owned street railway service within the city limits in the fall of 1921, the Yonge route from the city limits through Newtonbrook and on to Lake Simcoe was taken over by Ontario Hydro. In 1927 operation of the entire line was turned over to the TTC. This continued until March 16, 1930, when the plug was pulled and all radial service on Yonge ended. However, several communities along the route were unhappy with the bus service that was substituted and arranged to have the radials between the city limits and Richmond Hill reinstated. The big cars continued to rumble through Newtonbrook and on to Richmond Hill until the service was abandoned once again, this time on the pretext of saving electricity at a time when post–Second World War development had caused a shortage of electric power.

Viaduct: A Mammoth Project

Over the years great plans have been proposed for various areas along Toronto's waterfront. Some, like the creation of the western beaches out to the Humber River, the broad Lake Shore Boulevard, and the Toronto Harbour Industrial District (now the Port Lands), came to fruition and in doing so changed the look of the city. Others, such as Harbour City—that would have seen Toronto Harbour filled with floating apartments—and the plan to turn part of the Toronto Islands into a shopping centre, were thankfully scuttled. Today a whole series of projects to improve the waterfront are in either the planning or building stages.

Interestingly, it was in 1930 that one of the most controversial waterfront projects in the city's long history came to fruition with the official opening of what was called the Esplanade Viaduct. This mammoth project, built at an estimated cost of $40 million, was conceived as a way to elevate the railway corridor 18 feet above street level thereby ridding the city of the dangers presented by the numerous tracks that cut citizens off from their waterfront.

The first set of tracks had originally been put in place along the water's edge in the 1850s. Over the ensuing years they had been added to many times so that by the turn of the twentieth century getting to and from the Islands' ferries or the lake boat docks using one of the city's main north-south streets was a severe and sometimes deadly challenge.

Although the great fire of 1904 dealt a devastating, and some thought fatal, blow to Toronto (Hamilton would surely succeed Toronto as Ontario's major business centre), the rubble it left along the south side of Front Street between Bay and York was soon selected by the all-powerful railways as the site of a new Union Station. To coordinate the construction and all that it entailed, Toronto Terminal Railways was created, and while it took nearly 15 years to build the station, the viaduct by which the

Weighing 656,365 pounds, Canadian National Railway's giant steam engine No. 4100 was used to test the structural strength of the new cross-waterfront railway viaduct.

trains would come and go took even longer. That was because the project was both complex (involving, as it did, three different railway companies, the Canadian Northern and Grand Trunk—which eventually amalgamated to become Canadian National—and the Canadian Pacific) and required a seemingly endless array of government officials. But what really kept things on hold was the refusal of the railways to participate in what was becoming a very, very expensive project.

In fact, at one stage in the negotiations Canadian Pacific decided to have nothing more to do with the downtown station and its viaduct. CPR would build its own station adjacent to its rail line, which crossed Yonge near Summerhill Avenue. The company relocated to its North Toronto Station in 1916 where operations continued until it moved back to the new Union Station that had been opened, officially at least, in the summer of 1927.

The fact that the viaduct had yet to be completed meant that most passengers continued to use the old, rundown Union Station located farther west on Front. Finally, on January 21, 1930, two passenger trains—CPR's service from Peterborough and CNR's service from Peterborough and Stratford—entered the station on the city's new viaduct. Later that spring the underpasses on York, Bay, and Yonge streets were opened to traffic and pedestrians.

Now thousands continue to get to and from work, home, and the Islands' ferries via roads threaded under this historic waterfront project.

FILEY Fact

Union Station is actually the third city railway station with that title. To be a "union" station it had to serve more than one railway. As a result, the first "real" Union Station was located at Front and Bay and was used by the Grand Trunk and Great Western railways. The second was located south of Front and west of York and served the Grand Trunk and the new Canadian Pacific Railway. The third, and present Union Station, is now used by VIA Rail and GO Transit.

Toronto's Other Main Street

Have you ever wondered why Toronto has a Main Street several miles east of its real main thoroughfare, Yonge Street? The answer is simple. It was on December 15, 1908, that the City of Toronto grew in size by nearly 600 acres following the annexation of the Town of East Toronto. This community, on the eastern outskirts of the recently established City of Toronto, had first been settled sometime in the 1850s. Originally nothing more than a few houses and shops, the community located in the sprawling Township of York grew slowly in and around the intersection of the dusty east-west trail that connected it with the city some miles to the west, a thoroughfare now known as Danforth Avenue, and the hamlet's own north-south street, another dusty trail that naturally enough was dubbed Main Street, since that's exactly what it was.

As the years went by, the locals grew tired of the lack of attention they were getting from the township whose officials were often too busy with other matters to pay much attention to their needs. In frustration the citizens petitioned the province to permit the community to be accorded village status. If granted, that would allow increased independence with an elected council to administer to its own needs.

The request was approved and came into effect on January 1, 1888. The newly incorporated Village of East Toronto initially had a population of about 800, with that number increasing dramatically over the next few years, thanks in great measure to the presence of the nearby railway yards. In 1903 the village became a town, a status it then held until December 15, 1908, when, with a population of 4,800, the Town of East Toronto vanished into the history books to become part of the City of Toronto's Ward One.

One remnant of the ancient hamlet was the retention of the name of one of its original thoroughfares. That's why there's still a Main Street several miles east of Yonge, Toronto's original main street.

Looking south on the Main Street Bridge over the railway tracks south of Danforth Avenue in the early 1900s. The Gerrard Street intersection is in the distance.

The view south on
Main Street in 2005.

12

Toronto Waterfront

On the Waterfront

Did you ever dig for buried treasure when you were young? You know, get out the pail and shovel and dig in the backyard or along the beach in front of the cottage, hoping to find who knows what. Well, forget about the backyard and the beach as places to excavate and try your hand along Toronto's waterfront. Of course, the waterfront I'm referring to is the one that, before years and years of landfilling pushed the water's edge out into Toronto Harbour, could be found just south of Front Street.

As the recent dig at the foot of Bathurst Street proves, there are still some great treasures to be found scattered along the city's old shoreline. To be sure, the remnants of the old Queen's Wharf are only the latest finds for, as some may recall, dozens of neat old things like bottles, utensils, pieces of pottery, and even a cannonball (though whether it was fired in anger or was simply a paperweight was never determined) were found when the excavation work for the SkyDome (now Rogers Centre) was underway. Many of the artifacts were incorporated into a small museum that was part of the "SkyDome Story" when the place opened in 1989. An item I remember particularly well was a century-old condiment bottle that still gave off the odour of mustard.

Remnants of the old Queen's Wharf recovered during excavation.

When the old waterfront near the present Bay Street–Lake Shore Boulevard West intersection was being probed in early 1997 for the foundations of the new Air Canada Centre, the wooden "bones" of an ancient Great Lakes sailing vessel were discovered. I don't recall any steps being taken to preserve those relics.

As for the old wharf that was recently unearthed just west of the Bathurst Street–Lake Shore Boulevard corner, it was erected in 1833, one year before the Town of York became the City of Toronto. At the time its primary use was as a depot for goods destined for the nearby military garrison occupying what we know today as

Fort York. In 1837 the wharf was enlarged and given a name, the Queen's Wharf, in tribute to young Victoria, who in that same year became queen of Great Britain and Ireland. To aid nighttime navigation into the harbour, a lantern was set up at the west end of the wharf, which in turn was replaced in 1861 by a new lighthouse.

In 1906, while attempting to navigate the dangerous waters of the old and original Western Channel, the steam barge *Resolute* sank with the loss of six lives. That event, combined with several other near disasters, prompted officials to construct a new channel— the current Western Channel—1,300 feet farther south, which was ready for ship traffic in 1911. In the process of creating this new waterway, the old channel, along with its historic Queen's Wharf, were buried under tons of dirt and debris only to be unearthed during construction of a modern condominium tower. The name Queen's Wharf Condos has a nice ring to it. What do you think?

In an extraordinary example of preserving the past for the future, the old Queen's Wharf lighthouse was moved to its present location south of the former Molson plant in 1929.

Old Harbour Revisited

It would seem that the Toronto Island Airport ... oops, I should say the Toronto City Centre Airport ... remains as controversial as ever. In fact, during a recent foggy spell, much was made of the need to divert some of the Porter Airlines departures and arrivals to Pearson Airport. That's an interesting turn of events because when the Island Airport was built in the late 1930s a second airport in the countryside near the farming village of Malton northwest of the city was also under construction. That one (now called Toronto Pearson International) was to serve as a backup facility just in case the main airport on the Islands was ... wait for it ... fogged in!

Historically, the reason we have an Island Airport controversy is a result of something that happened on November 22, 1906. On that day a tremendous storm struck the Toronto area. The high winds and rough water created by the storm were so brutal that the steam barge *Resolute*, which was bound for the Port of Toronto from Erie, Pennsylvania, with a cargo of 430 tons of hard coal, was unable to navigate the city's old Western Channel that led from the lake into Toronto Harbour. Because the waterway was shallow, narrow, and badly maintained, the trip through it was virtually impossible in bad weather.

While attempting to ride out the raging storm, the heavily laden barge began taking on water. Suddenly, the *Resolute* overturned, spilling her crew of 12 into the swirling waters. Only half of that number was rescued. Six people drowned within sight of one of the safest harbours anywhere on the Great Lakes.

Many criticized those that allowed the channel to get into such a state and for allowing such a disaster to occur. It took several months for the federal government to react, but finally the minister of public works announced that a new, deeper, and wider Western Channel would be constructed 1,300 feet south of the old waterway. Work commenced in 1908 and was opened to navigation in early 1911.

It is the presence of this 400-foot-wide waterway that has resulted in the constant arguing as to how to get to and from the Island Airport. Now if they had only listened to the Toronto Harbour Commission's chief engineer, the late Jack Jones who, many years ago, suggested creating a new Western Channel south of the airport and filling in the old waterway. That would have resulted in the airport being part of the mainland. Problem solved.

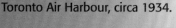

Toronto Air Harbour, circa 1934.

Island Fantasy

Benjamin Franklin once said "in this world nothing can be said to be certain except death and taxes." Well, Ben, one more thing that you can add to your "certain" list is that the argument over the future of Toronto's Island Airport will go on forever.

It all started in 1935 when, as the *Evening Telegram* trumpeted in the headline on the front page of its February 8 edition, "Toronto to Provide Land, Ottawa to Spend Million for Modern Air Harbour."

This announcement foretold of a million-dollar scheme to build a new airport for the city on a stretch of land that was still referred to as simply the Sandbar on the south side of the Western Channel. We know that location today as part of Hanlan's Point.

The paper went on to describe Ottawa's plan for the project, indicating that as a result of spending $1 million the federal government believed the city would get "one of the finest airports on the American continent." To continue: "A certain amount of filling in will be necessary, but when completed 135 acres of land will be available. It is also proposed to build a tunnel beneath the Western Gap from the foot of Bathurst Street through which traffic will run. Whether the tunnel will be large enough for cars and streetcars is problematical."

When the tunnel didn't materialize, it became necessary to provide some kind of access, and in 1938 a former Montreal Harbour scow was pressed into service. It was fitted with a winch connected to steel cables that were affixed to either side of the Western Channel. Operating the winch allowed the scow to pull itself back and forth across the 400-foot-wide waterway. Up until the time the scow was retired in 1963 it had travelled nearly 50,000 miles and had gone nowhere.

For the next three years the new Toronto Islands ferry *Ongiara* was used to convey people to and from the airport. Then, in 1965, the Toronto Harbour Commission bought the former Prescott, Ontario, to Ogdensburg, New York, ferry *Maple City*, and it entered airport service the following year. Another St. Lawrence River ferry, *Windmill Point*, was added as backup in the early 1980s.

The Toronto Port Authority recently proposed purchasing a new ferry that would provide one of the shortest and, on occasion, roughest boat rides in the world.

TCCA1, the new Toronto City Centre Airport ferry, entered service with an unusual first trip on October 11, 2006.

Across the Water and into the Air

On October 11, 2006, a new ferry boat entered service on Toronto Bay. Well, not exactly on the bay but rather on the Western Channel, the 400-foot-wide channel that separates the Toronto City Centre Airport from the mainland. The new vessel, known as *TCCA1*, a name that hopefully will be changed someday to recognize some aspect of our city's rich history, is owned by the Toronto Port Authority and is the fourth craft to provide access to and from the airport.

Interestingly, had officials implemented the initial plans prepared in the mid-1930s for Toronto's new "air harbour" across the bay on what was still just a couple of long strips of land covered in scrub brush and weeds, there would be no need for an airport ferry today. That's because an integral part of the project was a vehicle tunnel that was to be constructed from the foot of Bathurst Street under the channel to a parking lot adjacent to the airport terminal building. In fact, so sure were city officials that the money for the tunnel as promised by the federal government would be forthcoming that they went ahead and authorized its construction. The heavy equipment moved in, but no sooner had work started when the Conservative R.B. Bennett government was defeated by William Lyon Mackenzie King's Liberals. The decision to give the money was quickly cancelled and the hole was filled in. Now what?

The first ferry to serve the needs of the new Port George VI Island Airport was simply a converted barge. It was in service from 1939 until the *Maple City* arrived in 1966.

Work on the air harbour continued, though by now the idea of it serving water-based aircraft had been modified so as to place the emphasis on land-based planes. As the opening day for what had now been identified as Port George VI Island Airport approached, there was still no way to get people, freight, or fuel across the channel. As a stopgap measure, a forlorn-looking barge was quickly modified to serve as the airport's new ferry. The motive power onboard was simply a pair of winches, each of which was connected to cables strung from one end of the barge to the airport dock and the other end to the dock on the mainland. Using one or the other of the winches, the barge was simply pulled back and forth across the 400-foot-wide channel. To alert vessels making their way through the channel to be on the lookout for the ferry (and more specifically its taut cable), an arm would be set to project from a tall semaphore located near the dock on the Islands' side of the channel.

The stopgap ferry remained in service for the next 24 years until it was replaced by a tug. In 1965 the *Maple City*, one of the ferries that ran between Prescott, Ontario, and Ogdensburg, New York, became available, following the opening of the new suspension bridge over the St. Lawrence River that connects those communities. In the early 1980s a second ferry, the *Windmill Point*, which had also provided ferry service between Prescott and Ogdensburg, came to Toronto after a stint on Lake Saint Clair. On October 11, 2006, the modern new Toronto City Centre Airport ferry *TCCA1* officially entered service.

Island Flights Take Off

Say, has the controversy over building a "fixed link" in the form of a bridge to the Toronto Island Airport finally gone away? What prompts me to ask is the fact that it was almost 70 years ago that the first airplane landed there. And with that historic event Toronto had finally entered the "aviation age." To be sure, the city already had several small airfields such as the one in Leaside and another out near Wilson and Dufferin in North York Township, but they had grass strips and wooden barns for offices, so you couldn't really call them airports.

However, when Harry McLean set the wheels of his Stinson Reliant down on the paved runway of the newly built airport situated on what had been a deserted sandbar on the other side of the Western Channel that fourth day of February 1939, Toronto finally entered aviation's big league.

Not only did the city have the modern airport on the Islands, but the Toronto Harbour Commission was also building one near the small farming community of Malton, a few miles northwest of the city. In fact, the THC was employing the same plans for its Malton control tower as were used for the one on the Islands. The difference was that the Malton facility would only be used if and when the main airport on the Islands was shut down due to inclement weather along the waterfront.

Interestingly, Harry McLean, who landed that first plane, was as controversial in his time as the new airport would become years later. Harry Falconer McLean was born in North Dakota in 1883 of Canadian parents. After attending high school and business college south of the border, McLean moved to Canada where he entered the construction business. He worked on a variety of small jobs in various parts of the country, eventually taking on larger and more expensive projects. Some of his contracts included the Ontario Northland Railway, the Abitibi Canyon dam and power plant, and the Canadian Pacific Railway tunnel under the Plains of Abraham in Quebec City. On the subject of tunnels, McLean also worked on the original Lincoln Tunnel beneath the Hudson River in New York City.

It was a busy time at the Toronto Island Airport when this postcard image was produced, circa 1940.

It was calculated by those who worked for McLean that over a 40-year period his various companies carried out more than $400 million in construction contracts. It was once said of this true "builder" of Canada that if asked he would have bid on moving the Rocky Mountains, and if successful, would have moved them.

As successful and wealthy as he was, McLean was also, how should I say, a bit unusual. Once, while visiting Toronto's King Edward Hotel, a waiter tried to "pad" the lunch bill. Discovering the inaccuracy, McLean grabbed the poor fellow by the collar and dangled him out the 17th-floor window. Then, putting him back on his feet as if nothing had happened, he gave the shaken man a $100 tip.

While on business trips McLean would often and without warning open the window of his hotel room and shower the streets below with $100 bills. In November

1943, while visiting Toronto's Christie Street Military Hospital, he wandered the wards handing out large wads of money to astonished bed-ridden veterans.

Oh, and McLean liked to drink. Once, after being found inebriated in a public place in Sydney, Nova Scotia, he spent the night in the local lock-up. After being released, he sent the police a cheque for $5,000, suggesting they use the money to clean up the cells.

McLean's unusual habit of giving away money anonymously soon had the newspapers referring to him as the mysterious "Mr. X." And even when his identity was discovered, the money kept flowing. He gave away so much cash (some reports suggest the total exceeded $3 million) that when he died in his Merrickville, Ontario, residence in April 1961, he had only $75 in his wallet.

Toronto Bay's Slow Roller

Coincident with the unveiling of the replica at the Toronto Aerospace Museum, Downsview Park, I wrote about the development of the Avro Arrow, one of the most remarkable aircraft in the history of Canadian aviation. Many people have speculated that if the Arrow project had been allowed to continue the plane would still be far in advance of any military aircraft flying today. But because of the federal government's intercession that bleak Friday in February 1959, at which time the project was cancelled, we'll never know whether that supposition would have proved true.

Now, as spectacular as the Arrow was during its all-too-short lifespan in the late 1950s, there was a much earlier Canadian invention that was, to put it kindly, a total flop. Fred Knapp, a lawyer and inventor living in Prescott, Ontario, was sure his "roller boat" would conquer the

Frozen in the ice of Toronto Bay this remarkable photo of Knapp's "roller boat" shows the mechanism that kept the inner cylinder containing freight or passengers horizontal while the larger outer cylinder revolved as it rolled across the water. (Royal Canadian Yacht Club Archives)

problem passenger and freight vessels had with heavy seas. His invention would simply roll over the waves while the freight and/or passengers travelled in comfort inside a non-revolving inner cylinder.

Built in 1897 at the Polson Iron Works yard at the foot of Sherbourne Street—a company that built the Islands ferry *Trillium* 13 years later—Knapp's roller boat made several attempts to prove itself on Toronto Bay. Unfortunately, while Knapp's creation did roll across the bay more than a century ago, the rate at which it did was so slow as to make any successful commercial use of the craft unlikely. A number of modifications were made to the roller boat, but there was little improvement in the vessel's operating characteristics. Eventually, the 110-foot-long, 23-foot-diameter steel hulk was simply abandoned.

As the years passed and the city's new waterfront was being thrust farther into Toronto Bay, poor Mr. Knapp's invention was simply buried in the muck and mud where it no doubt still rests, waiting for the day it's unearthed.

13

Toronto Famous and Celebrated

And the Bands Played On

CELEBRATE
NEW YEAR'S EVE
AT
CASA LOMA
Music by Canada's Sensational New Maestro
ART HALLMAN
AND HIS ORCHESTRA
Vocals by LORRAINE McALLISTER   Dancing 9 Until 2 a.m.
HATS - HORNS - NOVELTIES - PRIZES
Tickets Now Selling $6 Per Couple—Phone KI. 0700
DANCING TONIGHT
ART HALLMAN   AND HIS ORCHESTRA
Saturday Broadcast CBL, 11 p.m.-11.30 p.m., Coast to Coast
SEE THE LARGEST TREE IN THE FOREST

Of all the columns I've written, those that receive the most reaction are the ones that deal with the big bands and dance halls of more than a half-century ago. Bands like those led by Stan Porch, Joe DeCourcy, Jack Evans, Cy McLean, and Pat Riccio, and dance halls such as the Silver Slipper, the Palace Pier, the Palais Royale (currently undergoing a remarkable renaissance), the Club Embassy and, of course, Toronto's much-treasured Casa Loma.

It was at Casa Loma that Bennie Louis and the legendary Mart Kenney repeatedly occupied the bandstand. However, if I were to guess who was the most frequent bandleader to play the castle, and base that assumption on the names mentioned in the letters and emails I receive, that person would have to be Art Hallman.

It was my good fortune to meet Art when I worked at the Canadian National Exhibition back in the 1970s and 1980s. One year my task was to revive the Big Band Dance Tent, something that had been a popular feature of the fair many years before. To ensure the Dance Tent idea worked, I called Moxie Whitney of Royal York Hotel fame and, of course, Art Hallman. That's when I first met a man whose performing and arranging styles had earned him the nickname "Canada's Glenn Miller."

Several years later I had the chance to initiate a similar program in the Seniors' Pavilion in the former Railways, then Music, Building at the west end of the grounds. This time Art called me, and even though he was now into his seventies, he asked (and this I won't forget) if I could get him some work.

Of course I could. Everyone knew Art Hallman. He would be perfect!

Amazingly, throughout the heat of that year's Ex, Art made his way to and from the old Music Building by bus, subway, and streetcar from his home in Thornhill.

One day I asked Art if I could interview him and would he mind telling his many fans how he got started in the music business. The next day he showed up with all the pertinent details nicely written down, ready for our interview. That document is one of the most treasured items in my collection. I offer it here just as Art had prepared it:

I was born in Kitchener, Ontario, and later moved to Vancouver, B.C. At the age of eight I began taking classical piano lessons which lasted for a period of 10 years. At age 21 I had my first professional engagement as a piano player in a band on a CNR summer cruise ship sailing from Vancouver to Alaska. Two years later, I joined radio station CJOR as the staff pianist and singer. In 1932, I was hired by the Mart Kenney band and became a part of the original Seven Western Gentlemen as featured vocalist, pianist, sax player and arranger. In 1941, I moved to Toronto with the band and did engagements at the Royal York and Brant Inn. Perhaps the most vivid memories of those years were the many coast to coast tours across Canada playing at the wartime service camps. It was 1945 when I formed my own band in Toronto made up of fourteen musicians. My first engagement was at Casa Loma which at the time was a favourite meeting place for the high school and university students. Radio broadcasts from Casa Loma started in November 1945 over the CBC Network. For 10 years I did a sing-a-long show from an open air bandstand at Sunnyside that drew large crowds every Sunday night. During the 60s, I acted as choral director on the Juliette TV show. My band has made many appearances at the CNE and for over 30 years I have been performing at the Jubilee Ballroom in Oshawa. I continue to do conventions, private dances, etc., at the major hotel ballrooms in Toronto. I've been most fortunate in my musical career and I still love to perform.

Art Hallman passed away on December 5, 1994.

Oscar's First Toronto Show

Recently, the world lost one of its finest jazz musicians with the death of Montreal-born Oscar Peterson. He passed away on December 23, 2007, in his Mississauga, Ontario, home at the age of 82. After Oscar's death, the media was full of stories as well as sound bites and video clips that covered his six decades at the keyboard. But none (at least none I heard or saw) chronicled Oscar's very first appearance in Toronto. So I did a little hunting and here's what I found.

Oscar Peterson's initial visit to Toronto occurred on November 6, 1945, when the six-foot-two-inch, 20-year-old arrived in town to make a personal appearance in the record department on the sixth floor of Simpson's Queen Street store (now The Bay) where he signed his various RCA Victor 78 rpm records that included "I Got

Rhythm" and on the flip side (when was the last time you heard that term?) "Sheik of Araby." Simpson's newspaper ad promoting Peterson's visit described him as "Canada's Own Prince of Swing" who makes "the dizzy digits produce piano swing that's really something ... and is cheerfully modest about the whole thing."

Another four months would pass before Peterson made his next public appearance in Toronto and again it was in Simpson's record department. A couple of his new Victor records—this time including "The 'C' Jam Blues" and "If I Could Be with You One Hour Tonight"—were available for 75 cents each. "Phone and out-of-town orders filled, call Trinity 8111."

Later that evening Peterson made a surprise visit to the Home Service Community Centre at 556 Bathurst Street. Here he performed for a group of 100 or so teenagers who made that old building their headquarters. A number of older people also showed up to hear what this thing called swing was all about. The session was described as "short but torrid." A reporter covering the event wrote: "There was no pretense about Oscar, but there is an awful lot of dignified affability and size."

However, the main reason for the young man's visit to Toronto was to give a recital on the evening of March 7, 1946, at Massey Hall—his first public performance in the city. The concert by "Canada's Sensational 20-year-old Piano Stylist" featured a program of modern and classical music with rhythm accompaniment. Reserved seat tickets were priced from 90 cents to $2.40.

Over the years, Peterson returned to Toronto on numerous occasions, and a check of the entertainment columns in the local papers of the early 1950s reveals some of the locations at which he appeared: the Paddock Tavern on Queen Street West, the Club Norman at 12 Adelaide Street East, the Colonial Tavern on Yonge (opposite Eaton's), and the Town Tavern on Queen Street just east of Yonge. Then, in the fall of 1955, Peterson returned to Massey Hall to star with such greats as Ella Fitzgerald, Gene Krupa, Stan Getz, Dizzy Gillespie, and Illinois Jacquet in "Jazz at the Philharmonic."

Canada's Oscar Peterson had made the big time, and the rest is history!

While on the subject of music, many readers will remember hearing their favourite musicians at Toronto dance halls that are now just memories, places like

NOW — IN TORONTO — OSCAR PETERSON. CANADA'S SENSATIONAL 20-YEAR-OLD PIANO STYLIST To Present a MODERN AND CLASSICAL PROGRAMME WITH RHYTHM ACCOMPANIMENT. MASSEY HALL, TONIGHT AT 8.30. Tickets 90c, $1.20, $1.80, $2.40. On Sale at Massey Hall, King Edward Hotel, Monday's Ticket Office—All Seats Reserved the Silver Slipper (later renamed Club Kingsway), the Embassy on Bloor Street West, Sunnyside's Club Esquire (later the Top Hat), and the recently restored Palais Royale. Arguably the most popular of all was the Palace Pier. To be constructed on the west bank of the Humber River where the watercourse flowed into Lake Ontario, this "world class" pleasure pier would, as described in a flowery prospectus released in 1927 by its developer the Provincial Improvement Corporation, "earn substantial profits for its investors who purchased shares being offered at $10 each (in units of 100)."

Unfortunately, and for a variety of reasons (the Great Depression being but one), things didn't turn out exactly as the developers had planned or the investors had hoped. In fact, the quarter-mile-long pier that appeared in those 1927 sketches didn't open for another 15 years, and when it did, it was a mere 300-foot-long auditorium called the Strathcona Palace Pier Roller Rink.

It wasn't long before the big bands discovered the place, and soon fans were dancing to the music of Harry James, the Dorseys, Duke Ellington, and of course, Canada's own Trump Davidson and Bert Niosi. Over the years religious revival meetings, wrestling and boxing matches, country and western shows, as well as trade shows of various types were also featured at the Palace Pier. But it all came to an end in early January 1963 when a firebug torched this one-time city landmark.

That Miller Sound

There was certainly a hot time in this old town on the evening of January 23, 1942. The reason for all the excitement was the fact that the legendary Glenn Miller and His Band, at the time the most popular in the entire world, were in Toronto to perform at the Mutual Street Arena. The location of Miller's first, and as it would turn out only, visit to Toronto was a barn of a building that had been constructed back in 1912 as an opera house, with one of its major investors being Henry Pellatt, the "Lord of Casa Loma." Known back then as simply the Arena, the place opened in early October with a huge six-day music festival. However, it wasn't long before the shareholders realized that with the public's fascination with hockey there was a lot of money to be made by converting the place into a hockey rink. Alterations were done quickly, and on Christmas night 1912 the Toronto Blueshirts took on the Canadiens from Montreal only to lose the first professional hockey game ever played in the building 9–5. During the ensuing years, a succession of professional hockey teams played in the rink, first the Blueshirts, then the Arenas, the St. Patricks, and in 1927, the newly created Toronto Maple Leafs (actually, all these teams were the same franchise under different ownership). The last team was so popular that its owner, Connie Smythe, decided to build a new and larger rink, and on November 12, 1931, his club played its first game in Maple Leaf Gardens. Like the Blueshirts did in their first game in the Arena, the Leafs lost.

With the move of Smythe's team to its new rink, the Arena, now renamed Mutual Street Arena for the thoroughfare on which it fronted (a street that got its name since it was laid out as a mutual driveway between two old properties), changed its focus and became home to numerous consumer and trade shows as well as the Toronto venue for many of the big American dance bands.

This then was the building that would have the distinction of being the only place that Glenn Miller ever played in Toronto and one of only two locations anywhere in Canada. (The day after his Toronto visit Miller and the boys went to London, Ontario, where they performed at the old London Arena before they returned to the United States.)

So popular was the Miller sound that within days of the newspaper announcement of the Toronto visit all 5,000 tickets were gone. Today's "art" of ticket scalping isn't new, for on the night of the performance the $1.50 tickets were going for as much as $5 apiece. There was even a notice in the papers telling fans still searching for tickets to be wary of counterfeit versions being offered for sale.

Glenn disappeared in December 1944 while flying from England to France in a Canadian-built plane flown by an ex-Royal Canadian Air Force pilot. While Miller obviously never returned to this country, his band, under the direction of a variety of leaders, did on many occasions.

In 1962 Mutual Street Arena underwent major renovations. As The Terrace, it quickly became popular with roller skaters and curlers until 1990 when it was demolished. Condos now stand on the site of Glenn Miller's one and only Toronto appearance.

Edward and the Ex

One of the most popular members of the royal family ever to visit Canada was Edward, the Prince of Wales, the man who became King Edward VIII but who decided, after spending less than a year on the throne, to marry American Wallis Simpson instead.

One of the prince's visits took place in August 1919 and included a stopover in Toronto. With commercial radio still a few years away, local television not making an appearance in Canada until 1952, and the Internet many decades in the future, the media of the day consisted solely of newspapers (not counting silent movies). Full coverage of the visit began during Edward's arrival in Quebec City. Then, toward the end of the month, it was Toronto's turn.

The prince arrived in Toronto early in the morning of August 25, 1919, on a special Canadian Pacific train. He first visited Government House in Rosedale, followed by a quick visit to the Ontario Parliament Buildings. Then it was down to the Canadian National Exhibition where before thousands of people the future king officially opened the annual fair.

Two days later the prince did something no one expected. With the horrors of the Great War still fresh in people's minds, Edward decided to take an unscheduled automobile tour of the city because, as he said, "he wanted to meet the ordinary people who did the dirty work in defeating the enemy."

This tour was taken in Sir John Eaton's Rolls-Royce automobile, "Yellowbird," and included visits to High Park, the Earlscourt area of town, and Prospect Cemetery where the prince planted a memorial tree. His car then made its way eastward and across the newly opened Bloor Street Viaduct, which connected the city with neighbourhoods out the Danforth.

While it's not known whether the prince made any comments about the mile-long structure, Toronto city council admired Edward so much that on September 3 it decreed that henceforth that structure would be officially known as the Prince Edward Viaduct, a title it still bears but which is usually forgotten in favour of its original name, the Bloor-Danforth Viaduct.

Eight months later the Prince of Wales returned to Toronto, this time accompanied by his younger brother, George, the Duke of Kent, and on August 30, 1927, they dedicated the newly constructed Eastern Entrance to the CNE grounds. This new entrance had been proposed several years earlier when it became apparent that the ever-increasing crowds headed for the annual fair needed another way inside in addition to the existing main entrance located at the foot of Dufferin Street nearly a mile to the west.

It was decided that with 1927 to be celebrated nationwide as the country's Diamond Jubilee of Confederation Year—celebrating the 60 years that had passed since Canada's first four provinces confederated in 1867—now was the perfect time to create a wonderful new "triumphant Eastern Entrance." Naturally enough, it would be called the Diamond Jubilee of Confederation Gates. However, with the two royal princes having agreed to officially dedicate the new structure during their Canadian visit, it didn't take long for that rather awkward name to be altered. And so it was that on August 30, 1927, and in the presence of Prince Edward and Prince George, the city's newest landmark was dedicated as the Princes' Gates.

The Prince of Wales returned to Toronto, and the CNE, in 1927, this time accompanied by his brother, Prince George. Here Edward is seen cutting the obligatory ribbon as he dedicates the new Princes' Gates. To the right is CNE President John J. Dixon; to the left Prince George chats with Ontario Lieutenant Governor W.D. Ross. (CNE Archives)

Marilyn Buoyed Our Hearts

If you were born in the mid-1950s and your name is Marilyn, there's a very good chance you were named in honour of Marilyn Bell, the 16-year-old, Toronto-born schoolgirl who became the first person to swim across Lake Ontario.

Marilyn was born in Toronto's St. Joseph's Hospital on October 19, 1937. As a teenager, she loved to swim and received much of her early training as a member of Alex Duff's Dolphinette Club, which practised at the now-demolished Oakwood pool not far from the busy St. Clair–Oakwood Avenue corner. Later

FILEY *Fact*

On May 22, 1939, Torontonians celebrated the arrival of their beloved king and queen, George VI and Elizabeth. It was believed by many that this visit was designed to ensure that when Adolf Hitler made his move against England, Canadians would be unhesitating in coming to the aid of the mother country. If nothing else, the outbursts of loyalty and devotion shown toward the royal couple by the citizens of the nation's principal English-speaking city during their one-day visit confirmed that. When the time came a few months later, Canadians by the thousands were in the thick of the war. Arriving at the North Toronto railway station early on the morning of May 22, the whirlwind tour took in visits to the University of Toronto, the Parliament Buildings, City Hall, Riverdale Park, Woodbine, and the Christie Street Military Hospital. Late in the day the couple boarded a special train to continue their cross-Canada tour.

she joined the Lakeshore Swimming Club, where she caught the eye of the irascible Gus Ryder.

Marilyn was still a student at Loretto College on Brunswick Avenue when she got it into her head that world-famous marathon swimmer Florence Chadwick wasn't the only person who could successfully complete the 23-mile crossing of Lake Ontario from the Wilson, New York, Coast Guard station to the Canadian National Exhibition waterfront.

Swimming across Lake Ontario, which had never been done before, was the challenge presented to the American swimmer by CNE officials as they sought to boost attendance at the 1954 celebration of the annual fair. If she succeeded, Florence would receive a cash prize of $10,000; if she failed, she would get just enough to cover her expenses. Either way the Ex couldn't lose. That $10,000 prize would be easily recovered from the 50-cent entrance fee handed over by each of the thousands of extra visitors at the Ex who were eager to witness the American swimmer make history.

As the Exhibition dates approached, Chadwick's participation in the cross-lake swim was finally confirmed. Most believed that if she couldn't do it, no one could. After all, this was *the* Florence Chadwick, two-time conqueror of the English Channel.

Young Marilyn had few credentials to suggest she had any chance of completing the gruelling crossing. Sure, under the tutelage of her coach, Gus Ryder, the youngster had done well in a few aquatic events, the most impressive being the 1953 Atlantic City Marathon, where she became the first woman (and seventh overall) to finish the 26-mile event. But that swim was around an island and it was only 26 miles in length. For most of the Lake Ontario swim she would be out of sight of land, and it would be six miles longer.

Crowds of well-wishers greet Marilyn Bell as she is paraded through New Toronto in her new convertible, which was given to her by the Austin Car Company. Her coach, Gus Ryder, is in the light-coloured suit. Beside him in the back seat is Robert Saunders, CNE president and former Toronto mayor.

Spurred on by the CNE's decision to limit the cross-lake challenge to a single competitor, and an American at that, plus an arrogant statement that even if the young hometown swimmer was successful (a highly unlikely possibility) there would be no prize money from the Exhibition, Marilyn decided to give it her best try.

Everyone cheered as Chadwick entered the cold lake on the evening of September 8, 1954. Minutes later Marilyn, too, was on her way, only noticed by her mother, father, coach, and a few friends in her pace boat.

Soon the cold water proved to be too much for Chadwick and she was taken trembling from the lake. Everyone believed that what had become known far and wide as the marathon swimming event of the century was over.

Then someone yelled, "Look over there!" Sure enough, someone else was still churning through the water—young Marilyn Bell! For more than 20 hours Marilyn and the lake battled each other. Initially, Marilyn was in command, but as the hours passed, the lake appeared to take over. While the outcome of Marilyn's duel with Lake Ontario is now well known and a high point in Canadian history, the joyous conclusion was often very much in doubt at the time.

The whole story was nicely told in the CBC feature production *Heart: The Marilyn Bell Story* as well as in several documentary presentations. And something I've never been able to figure out: the government has never deemed her various sporting accomplishments as well as her work with handicapped children worthy of the Order of Canada. Go figure!

Statue Honours Mary Pickford

Born in a nondescript two-storey house at 211 University Avenue on April 8, 1893, Gladys Marie Smith was the eldest of three children. Her father, John, worked as a purser on the Toronto-Lewiston steamers, and one day, while boarding his ship in Toronto, his head struck an unseen overhead pulley.

A blood clot soon formed, and within hours the Smith family was fatherless. Shortly thereafter, Dr. G.B. Smith of the Hospital for Sick Children on College Street suggested to Gladys's mother that he and his wife would like to adopt Gladys. The little girl was all set to join the good doctor and his wife who promised her everything.

Gladys soon realized that the offer didn't include her sister and brother, Lottie and Jack. She cried and said, "No thanks," and insisted she would remain at home.

A couple of months later a boarder came to live with the Smiths. Manager of the Cummings Stock Company, the newcomer asked Mrs. Smith whether the girls would like to appear in one of the company's stage productions at the Princess Theatre on King Street (where University Avenue now cuts through). Gladys was five when she appeared on the stage for the first time, and she took to it like the proverbial duck to water.

It wasn't long before Gladys appeared regularly in feature presentations. In 1909 the 16-year-old (looking 12) Gladys and her mother met with big-time theatre producer David Belasco. He quickly recognized the little girl's potential and afterward suggested a name change.

Gladys suggested "Mary from Marie and Pickford was my grandmother's maiden name."

"Great!" exclaimed Belasco. "And by the way, Mary, you'll make your Broadway debut as Betty in *The Warrens of Virginia* on November 11, 1907."

And so the legend of "America's Sweetheart" was born.

For the next 23 years she reigned as queen of the silent screen. From her first "one-reeler," *The Lonely Villa* in 1909, Mary captured the hearts of theatregoers in 125 short features and 52 full-length films. Her screen farewell was in the 1933 film *Secrets* with Leslie Howard, C. Aubrey Smith, and another Canadian, Guelph's own Ned Sparks. Mary always remembered her early life in Toronto.

In fact, she was bothered periodically by a cough, which she called her "Eaton cough." When Mary was a child, her mother would occasionally leave the youngster in her pram while she shopped in Eaton's. Mary developed the croup, which became her "Eaton cough."

Mary Pickford and her second husband, Douglas Fairbanks, visited Toronto often.

The great actress and her second husband, Douglas Fairbanks, visited Toronto often, and every time they did the crowds that turned out to greet the famous Torontonian numbered in the thousands.

Mary Pickford died at her California residence, Pickfair, on May 29, 1979. Four years later a sculptured likeness of America's Sweetheart was unveiled by her last husband, Buddy Rogers. Located on the lawn of the Hospital for Sick Children, it stands, along with a commemorative Ontario Heritage Foundation plaque, not far from the site of the house at 211 University Avenue in which Mary was born.

Toronto Timeline

1750–59 Fort Rouillé (also known as Fort Toronto), a trading post, is established by the French. An outline of the fort and an obelisk mark the site at the present-day Canadian National Exhibition grounds.

1793 Town of York (later Toronto) is founded. The Garrison at York (Fort York) is established by Lieutenant Governor John Graves Simcoe.

1797 Upper Canada's original Parliament Building, King's Park, is erected near the corner of today's Front and Berkeley streets. A Church of England congregation is founded in the Town of York. On land given to the congregation, a small wooden church is eventually built. From this humble beginning comes the Cathedral Church of St. James, whose current building is begun in 1850 and completed in 1875.

1800 Population of Town of York is approximately 403.

1803 St. Lawrence Market opens as the community's first public market.

1813 Americans attack and burn Fort York and Upper Canada's Parliament during the War of 1812.

1818 In between Garrison Reserve and King's Park, a public promenade known as The Walks and Gardens is established.

1820 Parliament is rebuilt at the Berkeley Street location; four years later it burns down again.

1827 King's College is chartered.

1831 Windmill Line is established to check industrial sprawl.

1832 The Parliament of Upper Canada (Ontario) meets in its new building on the north side of Front Street west of Simcoe Street. Gooderham and Worts opens as Worts and Gooderham.

1834	March 6: City of Toronto created. March 27: First Toronto election— William Lyon Mackenzie becomes the city's first mayor.
1837	December 4: Upper Canada Rebellion begins with a march down Yonge Street.
1841	Regular service of gas streetlights initiated.
1844	The *Globe* (later the *Globe and Mail*) is founded.
1850	King's College becomes the University of Toronto.
1853	Walks and Gardens design plan by John Howard sees a grand public park along the lakeshore.
1853	South of Bay and Front streets, the first Toronto rail station is built on the lakeshore. Windmill Line is abandoned.
1856	Railway is relocated from Front Street to The Esplanade.
1858	Toronto Islands are created when a storm destroys the western peninsula. The original Union Station is constructed at the bottom of York Street.
1860	July 30: Toronto passes bylaw 322. Archery is no longer allowed in public places; snowballs are no longer allowed in public parks.
1861	September 11: First horse-drawn streetcar goes into service.
1870	Queen's Hotel opens where the Royal York Hotel stands today.
1873	Second Union Station is built.
1876	Toronto's population reaches 71,693.
1879	What becomes known as the Toronto Industrial Exhibition is held for the first time, precursor to the Canadian National Exhibition (CNE).
1892	Gooderham (Flatiron) Building is built, replacing Coffin Block (erected in 1845). First electric streetcar goes into service. The *Toronto Star* is founded.
1893	Queen's Park becomes home to new Parliament Buildings at top of University Avenue.

1894 Massey Hall opens; its debut concert takes place on June 14.

1899 September 18: *Old* City Hall opens.

1900 The Art Gallery of Ontario is founded by a group of private citizens as the Art Museum of Toronto. It is renamed the Art Gallery of Toronto in 1919 and then becomes the Art Gallery of Ontario in 1966.

1901 Toronto's population hits 205,857.

1904 April 19: Great Toronto Fire breaks out, destroying a large part of the city's downtown core.

1906–07 Alderman for Toronto Ward 4 William P. Hubbard serves as acting mayor. The son of freed slaves from Virginia, he becomes Toronto's first black deputy mayor.

1907 Construction is completed on the Beaux Arts–style Royal Alexandra Theatre. The Royal Alex is the oldest continuously operating legitimate theatre in North America.

1910 A plane flies over Toronto for the first time.

1911 To coordinate public works for urban industrial expansion, the Royal Harbour Commission is created. Construction begins on Casa Loma, Sir Henry Pellatt's palatial home.

1912 Waterfront Parks Plan is released, calling for parks encircling the Toronto Islands and the city's port. Only Coronation Park and the new and current Union Station see the light of day.

1913 The original St. Clair Avenue streetcar service on a private right-of-way starts.

1914 Construction begins on the third and final Union Station. Casa Loma is completed at an estimated cost of $3.5 million. The Royal Ontario Museum's original building opens.

1917 The Toronto Harbour Commission Building is completed. It sits on the edge of Toronto Bay.

1919 Marcus Garvey founds Toronto's Universal Negro Improvement Association Building at 355 College Street. Black musicians stayed here when many Toronto hotels didn't welcome blacks as patrons. The entire length of the new Prince Edward (Bloor) Viaduct is opened to all traffic from Sherbourne Street to Broadview Avenue.

1921   Toronto's population reaches 522,666. Toronto Transportation Commission (TTC) begins operation after its creation in 1920.

1922   Sunnyside Amusement Park opens west of the CNE grounds.

1926   Cold storage facility built; still known as Queen's Quay Terminal.

1927   February 17: Toronto Maple Leafs, the renamed Toronto St. Patricks, make their first appearance. August 6: Third Union Station opens. August 31: Princes' Gates at the CNE is officially opened by Edward, Prince of Wales (the future King Edward VIII), and Prince George, the Duke of Kent.

1928   Canada Malting Plant is built at the foot of Bathurst Street.

1929   Royal York Hotel opens—at the time it is the tallest building in the British Empire and the largest hotel, as well. Automotive Building, designed by local architect Douglas Kertland, is erected at the CNE.

1931   Toronto's population reaches 627,231. Immigrants represent almost 40 percent of the city's residents, the highest such proportion on the continent.

1932   Construction begins on the R.C. Harris Water Filtration Plant at Queen Street East and Victoria Park Avenue. The facility is completed in 1941. In 1992 the plant is named a National Historic Civil Engineering Site by the Canadian Society for Civil Engineering.

1933   August 16: Long, hot summer of bigotry and hate boils over in the form of the Christie Pits Riots.

1934   Battery Park and Coronation Park open to the public.

1938   A small residential community on the Toronto Islands is razed to the ground to make way for an island airport; the airport's existence has been debated ever since.

1939   At the foot of Bathurst Street a sandbar is remade into the Port George VI Airfield. It later becomes the Toronto City Centre Airport.

Malton Airport (later Toronto International, then Toronto Pearson International Airport) opens.

1947   June 19: TTC introduces electric trolley buses.

1948   City begins building Regent Park, Canada's first large-scale public housing project.

1949   September 16: Passenger ship SS *Noronic* is destroyed by fire while docked in Toronto's harbour, the worst disaster in the city's history—119 souls perish in the fire.

1951   Population of Metropolitan Toronto has passed one million.

1953   Metropolitan Toronto Act passed by Ontario, creating Municipality of Metropolitan Toronto, composed of the City of Toronto; the towns of New Toronto, Mimico, Weston, and Leaside; the villages of Long Branch, Swansea, and Forest Hill; and the townships of Etobicoke, York, North York, East York, and Scarborough. Metro Toronto's jurisdiction becomes effective in 1954.

1954   March 30: Yonge subway line, Canada's first subway, opens. September 8–9: Marilyn Bell, a 16-year-old schoolgirl, becomes the first person to swim across Lake Ontario. It takes her nearly 21 hours. October 15: Hurricane Hazel floods local rivers and kills 81 people.

1955   Goodbye South Parkdale—the neighbourhood is destroyed to make way for the Gardiner Expressway.

1956   Goodbye Sunnyside—the amusement park neighbourhood is destroyed to make way for the Gardiner Expressway.

1958   August 8: First phase of the Gardiner Expressway opens; Parkdale residents are cut off from the waterfront. Hockey Hall of Fame moves to Toronto from Kingston—its first permanent building opens at Exhibition Place in 1961. When it outgrows that location, it is relocated to a former Bank of Montreal building in downtown Toronto in 1993, where it remains today.

1959   Exhibition Stadium at the CNE opens. Construction of breakwater for the Outer Harbour, dubbed the Leslie Street Spit, begins. York University is founded.

1961   Jane Jacobs publishes *The Death and Life of Great American Cities*. Jacobs later migrates to the Annex neighbourhood from New York City. *Report on the Need for a Long-Range Waterfront Plan* is drafted by Metro planners. Mixed-use planning on waterfront kicks in. August 3: First stretch of the Don Valley Parkway (Bayview-Bloor interchange to Eglinton Avenue) opens to the public.

1963   February 28: Yonge-University subway line opens.

1965   September 13: *New* City Hall opens.

1966   February 26: Bloor-Danforth subway line opens.

1967   May 2: Toronto Maple Leafs win the Stanley Cup for the last time. May 27: GO Transit begins service.

1969   Old City of Toronto holds a referendum on full amalgamation of all the jurisdictions that make up Metro Toronto. Eighty-two percent of Torontonians vote yes. Nevertheless, the provincial government refuses to redraw the city's boundaries. September 27: Ontario Science Centre officially opens.

1970   Harbour City proposal calls for canal housing constructed in Lake Ontario.

1971   Ontario Place is built as the only element of Harbour City to be realized. July 3: Ontario Premier Bill Davis cancels the Spadina Expressway project. The *Toronto Sun* is founded. Population of Metropolitan Toronto passes two million.

1972   Harbourfront Centre opens.

1974   Metropolitan Toronto Zoo opens.

1976   June 26: Completed CN Tower opens. Toronto International Film Festival makes its debut.

1977   First Phase of Toronto Eaton Centre opens. April 7: Toronto Blue Jays play their first game in Exhibition Stadium against the Chicago White Sox; they win 9–5 amid snow.

1978   January 28: Spadina subway line opens.

1979 Bay Street Ferry Terminal begins operation alongside opening of Harbourside condominiums.

1983 Queen's Quay Terminal converted into condominiums on top floors, retail shops on bottom two floors.

1984 Metro Convention Centre opens for business.

1985 March 24: Scarborough Rapid Transit (RT) line opens.

1989 Spadina Roundhouse is demolished. SkyDome (now Rogers Centre) is built on rail lands.

1992 Toronto Blue Jays win the World Series.

1993 Blue Jays repeat, winning their second World Series in a row. May 26: Princess of Wales Theatre opens with a local production of *Miss Saigon*. The construction of the theatre is financed by Ed and David Mirvish. Besides the Princess of Wales, Mirvish Productions now owns the Canon Theatre (formerly the Pantages Theatre), the Panasonic Theatre (formerly the New Yorker Theatre), and the Royal Alexandra Theatre.

1995 November 3: Toronto Raptors bring the National Basketball Association to town with home opener at SkyDome against the New Jersey Nets. The Raptors win the game 94–79.

1998 Metropolitan Toronto is dissolved. Etobicoke, York, Scarborough, North York, East York, and Toronto amalgamate to form a single mega-City of Toronto. The *National Post* is founded.

1999 Toronto Waterfront Revitalization Corporation is established—job is to oversee planning for the Portlands, central waterfront, and East Bayfront. February 13: Toronto Maple Leafs play their last game at Maple Leaf Gardens. February 20: Maple Leafs play their first game at the Air Canada Centre.

2001 The length of the Gardiner Expressway between the Don Valley Parkway and Leslie Street is demolished.

2002 Yonge-Dundas Square is unveiled to the public. Toronto Windmill becomes the first wind turbine installed in a major North American urban city centre.

2003   Distillery District, located at the site of the Gooderham and Worts
         Distillery, opens for business. SARS outbreak afflicts Toronto. The
         city experiences a massive widespread power outage—the largest
         blackout in North American history, affecting nearly 10 million people
         in Ontario alone.

2006   Work begins on the revitalization of the Regent Park area—the project
         is expected to take 12 years to complete. Population of Toronto has
         passed 2.8 million.

2007   April 28: Major League Soccer's Toronto FC debuts at BMO Field
         against the Kansas City Wizards. FC loses 1–0. June 3: Royal Ontario
         Museum opens the Michael Lee-Chin Crystal, a distinctive new
         symbol of Toronto for the twenty-first century.

2008   Construction begins at 1 Bloor Street on the southeast corner of Yonge
         Street. The sleek new 80-storey building will become Canada's tallest
         residential condominium/hotel/retail complex. Massive propane
         explosions rock Wilson Avenue–Keele Street neighbourhood, forcing
         thousands of people to evacuate.

2009   Toronto celebrates the 175th anniversary of its incorporation in 1834.

Part Titles

...ntertime postcard from the early twentieth ...ry.

...ersity Avenue looking north from Queen ..., with the unfinished South African War ...orial at right.

...posal for the Sunnyside Palace Pier, which ...e the home of Trump Davidson and His ...stra for many years.

...ichard L. Hearn Generating Station is open ...siness in October 1951.

...vastation caused by Toronto's Great Fire ...4 was immense.

...d in 1895, the impressive cast-iron Temple ...g once stood at the corner of Richmond ...y streets.

...ntario Legislative Buildings, sometimes ...he "Pink Palace," at Queen's Park in all ...ardsonian Romanesque glory.

...d Serafin's 1950s conception of the ...loor subway interchange looking south ...nge Street on the right.

...in this circa 1925 postcard, the Canadian ...l Exhibition's third Grandstand was ...of many thrilling events, including ...es.

...south on Broadview Avenue from ...Street, circa 1912.

11 Toronto Neighbourhoods   Kingston Road looking west to Woodbine Avenue in 1908.

12 Toronto Waterfront   A 2006 artist's conception of the new Toronto City Centre Airport ferry connection. (Courtesy Toronto Port Authority)

13 Toronto Famous and Celebrated   Marilyn Bell meets her favourite singing group, The Four Lads, soon after her historic Lake Ontario swim.

Other Books by Mike Filey

Toronto Sketches 9:
The Way We Were
978-1-55002-613-9
$19.99

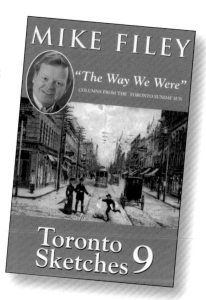

Toronto Sketches 8:
The Way We Were
978-1-55002-527-9
$22.99

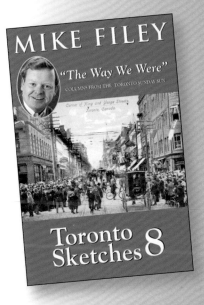

A Toronto Album 2: More Glimpses
of the City That Was
978-1-55002-393-0 $24.99

A photographic journey through
bustling Toronto from the late 1930s to
the early 1970s. Among the 100-plus
photographs is a quartet that shows
the remarkable changes to Toronto's
skyline over a half-century.

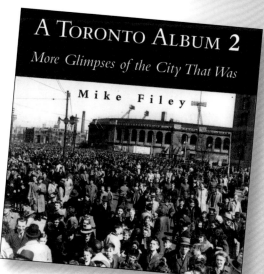

Of Related Interest

Unbuilt Toronto: A History of the City That Might Have Been

by Mark Osbaldeston
978-1-55002-835-5 $26.99

An exploration of the failed architectural dreams of Toronto and the surrounding area over four centuries.

Osgoode Hall: An Illustrated History

by John Honsberger
978-1-55002-513-2 $60.00

Of the many public buildings erected in pre-Confederation Canada and British North America, Osgoode Hall best encapsulates the diverse stylistic forces that shaped public buildings in the first half of the nineteenth century.

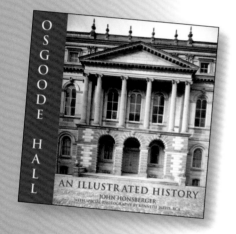

DUNDURN PRESS

www.dundurn.com

Tell us your story!
What did you think of this book?
Join the conversation at
www.definingcanada.ca/tell-your-story
by telling us what you think.

More Books by Mike Filey

A Toronto Album: Glimpses of the City That Was	978-0-88882-242-0	$24.99
Toronto Sketches: The Way We Were	978-1-55002-176-9	$16.99
More Toronto Sketches: The Way We Were	978-1-55002-201-8	$14.99
Toronto Sketches 3: The Way We Were	978-1-55002-227-8	$14.99
Toronto Sketches 4: The Way We Were	978-1-55002-248-3	$15.99
Toronto Sketches 5: The Way We Were	978-1-55002-292-6	$16.99
Toronto Sketches 6: The Way We Were	978-1-55002-339-8	$17.99
Toronto Sketches 7: The Way We Were	978-1-55002-448-7	$18.99
Discover & Explore Toronto's Waterfront	978-1-55002-304-6	$14.99
The TTC Story	978-1-55002-244-5	$19.99

Available at your favourite bookseller.